"Andrew Boa's experience as a campus leader taught h [barcode] munity for healing sexual brokenness. In *Redeemed Sexuality*, Bo discipleship that will help all kinds of strugglers encounter the risen Lord Jesus and experience his life-giving grace."
Philip Ryken, president, Wheaton College

"*Redeemed Sexuality* is just the book that needed to be written today—and Drew Boa did an amazing job writing it! The great strengths of this book are its practicality, applicability to both men and women, and focus on eighteen- to thirty-year-olds. If you're looking for a small group curriculum on sexual wholeness, buy this book immediately!"
John D. Foubert, author of *How Pornography Harms*

"'Sexual brokenness is no longer the exception among young Christians; it is the norm,' writes Drew Boa. We seem to be stuck in repeated cycles of sin, confession, repentance, sin, and then shame. I believe Boa's approach can break that cycle by focusing on spiritual formation for our sexuality through groups that build vulnerability, identity, and intimacy. In a pilot of this material, leaders witnessed breakthroughs for their students, who subsequently grew in spiritual authority. We need this book!"
Carolyn Carney, assistant regional director for spiritual formation, InterVarsity Christian Fellowship/USA

"One of the greatest hindrances to overcoming lust and addiction is isolation. We see this over and over, yet so many Christians think they can slay their sin without any help. I love *Redeemed Sexuality* because it incorporates one of our greatest weapons: the body of Christ. I expect great waves of freedom to sweep over the church as we get honest and purposeful in community."
Jessie Minassian, founder of LifeLoveandGod.com, author of *Unashamed: Overcoming the Sins No Girl Wants to Talk About*

"Struggles with sexual wholeness are as old as humanity, but the proliferation of mobile digital technology and the immediate access to pornography it allows has rewritten the rulebook for this generation. We can no longer ignore the epidemic of sexual brokenness young adults are facing. They are looking to their churches and Christian communities for help, but most lack the knowledge and resources to address the systemic sexual malformation evident today. Thankfully, *Redeemed Sexuality* has been created to help us address the deep roots of sexual brokenness with a holistic response. This curriculum honors the gravity of the struggle as well as the God-given dignity of the young people it is designed to help. That means avoiding simple answers or merely focusing on temporary behavioral changes. *Redeemed Sexuality* seeks deeper healing in the context of meaningful community. It is the right tool for our times."
Skye Jethani, author of *With: Reimagining the Way You Relate to God*

"*Redeemed Sexuality* offers a rare resource in today's Christian culture—a program for young adults to talk frankly in community about the pervasive issue of pornography and other forms of sexual brokenness. This guide is less about sin management and more an invitation to understand your story, your heart's holy desires, and especially the heart of God for redeeming the amazing gift of sexuality. This curriculum is well written by a man wise beyond his years. The Christian community needs to hear lots more from Andrew Boa."
Marnie C. Ferree, author of *No Stones: Women Redeemed from Sexual Addiction*, director of Bethesda Workshops, Nashville, Tennessee

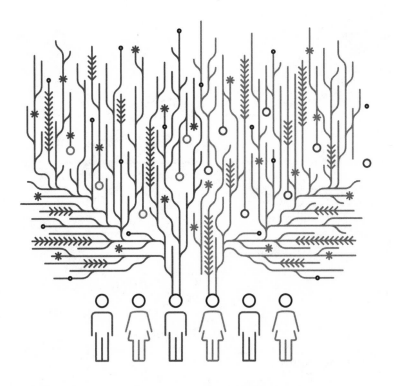

REDEEMED

SEXUALITY

Healing and Transformation in Community

12 SESSIONS

ANDREW A. BOA

IVP Connect

An imprint of InterVarsity Press
Downers Grove, Illinois

InterVarsity Press
P.O. Box 1400, Downers Grove, IL 60515-1426
ivpress.com
email@ivpress.com

InterVarsity Press® is the book-publishing division of InterVarsity Christian Fellowship/USA®, a movement of students and faculty active on campus at hundreds of universities, colleges, and schools of nursing in the United States of America, and a member movement of the International Fellowship of Evangelical Students. For information about local and regional activities, visit intervarsity.org.

All Scripture quotations, unless otherwise indicated, are taken from The Holy Bible, New International Version®, NIV®. Copyright © 1973, 1978, 1984, 2011 by Biblica, Inc.™ Used by permission of Zondervan. All rights reserved worldwide. www.zondervan.com. The "NIV" and "New International Version" are trademarks registered in the United States Patent and Trademark Office by Biblica, Inc.™

While any stories in this book are true, some names and identifying information may have been changed to protect the privacy of individuals.

Cover design: Faceout Studio
Interior design: Jeanna Wiggins
Images: male and female icons: © Visual Generation / Shutterstock Images
*   illustration: © Libellule / Shutterstock Images*

ISBN 978-0-8308-2127-3 (print)
ISBN 978-0-8308-8992-1 (digital)

Printed in the United States of America ∞

InterVarsity Press is committed to ecological stewardship and to the conservation of natural resources in all our operations. This book was printed using sustainably sourced paper.

Library of Congress Cataloging-in-Publication Data
A catalog record for this book is available from the Library of Congress.

P	28	27	26	25	24	23	22	21	20	19	18	17	16	15	14	13	12	11	10	9	8	7	6	5	4	3	2	1
Y	41	40	39	38	37	36	35	34	33	32	31	30	29	28	27	26	25	24	23	22	21	20	19	18	17

To Redeemed group leaders:

His grace is sufficient for you,

for his power is made perfect in weakness.

2 CORINTHIANS 12:9

CONTENTS

FOREWORD

William Struthers

When Drew Boa contacted me and asked to meet, I wondered what his intentions were. He wasn't a current or former student, so I was curious. When he invited me to preview a draft of the curriculum he was developing as part of his graduate training, I was intrigued.

Drew has taken his early works and reframed them into something exciting. Too often sexual curriculum takes on a military tone, as if we are constantly at war with our bodies, or—at a very minimum—at war with the sexual thoughts and desires that we do not want to entertain for any number of reasons. I think you will find that this is not what *Redeemed Sexuality* is about.

As a researcher and educator I usually put resources such as these into two categories. The first is (please pardon my college-level framework) a "Sex 101" view of sexuality that offers a list of dos and don'ts. These resources focus on behavior management and the mechanisms of reproduction, while ignoring the spiritual, emotional, and psychological realities many Christians wrestle with as they attempt to adhere to the teachings of Scripture.

The second is a "Theology/Philosophy of Sex 301" view that provides esoteric arguments offered by scholars who seem clinically distant and dispassionate from the realities of day-to-day life. They offer the promise of freedom from bondage but they do not always offer the means to jump from the 101 to the 301 level.

What I find helpful about *Redeemed Sexuality* is that it fits into the space between these two sets of resources—a practical 201 transition. It offers a distinctively Christian view of sexual development *and* a route forward to move deeper into a Christian virtue. It offers a bridge between the overly simplistic ways to manage sexual sin to a rich way of thinking of sexuality that offers freedom without stripping human sexuality of its vitality. I think you will find *Redeemed Sexuality* a welcome addition to the very muddied valley that so many Christians feel lost in.

AN INVITATION
TO THE BROKEN

Sexual brokenness is no longer the exception among young Christians; it is the norm. Internet porn, sexual assault and abuse, and overall sexual self-centeredness plague Christians and non-Christians alike, vandalizing God's beautiful gift of sexuality. Christians are called to value and celebrate sexuality as sacred and good, yet our sexuality is more often a source of fear, shame, or secret sin than love, joy, and intimacy with God and others. What was intended to be a place of holy connection and captivation has become a place of helpless captivity for countless people inside and outside the church.

How did this happen? Certainly the problem is not a lack of instruction—there have never been more books, sermons, and other resources available on the topic of sexuality than there are now. Most young Christians know the rules. They have been taught what to believe and how (not) to behave sexually. The real problem lies in a deficiency in our entire approach to the subject of sex. Growing up, most of us were taught that sexual purity meant "holding our breath" sexually until marriage, when we would finally be able to let it all out. We learned what to avoid sexually, but not what to pursue, missing out on the reason why God made us sexual beings: to draw us into deep intimacy with himself and others—married or not. This gap has left a generation of Christians ill-equipped to face complex sexual challenges and heal from sexual brokenness.

While many churches offer sexual education and advocate for purity, it's rare to find one that invites sexually broken people into an ongoing process of discipleship. Sexual discipleship is the daily process of training our sexual desires, attitudes, and actions. Unfortunately, the surrounding culture does a much better job of this than the church: shaping how we think, what we love, and what we pursue when it comes to sexuality. We have more than enough information about sexuality. What we need is for sexuality to be included as an integral part of our spiritual formation and discipleship.

Redeemed Sexuality is a resource for small group discipleship focused on sexuality. Suitable for men's or women's groups, this curriculum is specifically designed for college students and emerging adults who love Jesus but find themselves stuck in patterns of sexual brokenness. It aims to create a context where sexually broken people seek real acceptance and significance through the love of God in community instead of through sexually broken behaviors. It also offers a mature answer to the burning question of so many emerging adults: *As a single, unmarried Christian, what am I supposed to do with my sexual desires?* We are called to pursue intimacy with God and others; rather than reject our identity as sexual beings, we can embrace our identity as people who are created for holy love in healthy relationships.

Christianity offers us a mature view of sexuality: sex is not gross, but it's not God either. Sexuality is good, and it's a gift. Precisely because our sexuality is so good, God protects it with specific boundaries. He designed sexual union to take place within the context of marriage, and he forbids us to treat other people as sexual objects. We are called to cherish, protect, and honor the image of God in all people with our sexuality. Only then can we experience it as a gift instead of a burden.

A Christian view of sexuality frees us to celebrate sex without worshiping it. Because our sexuality is good, we are invited to pursue and enjoy intimacy with others, whether we are single, dating, or married. As a result, our job is neither to suppress nor to always satisfy our desires, but to surrender them in self-giving

love, just like the Father, Son, and Spirit have been doing since before the world began.

Whether you're part of a campus ministry, a Christian college, or a local church, I invite you on a journey—not just to sexual purity but to sexual maturity. This journey is a process of healing and transformation in community. In *Redeemed Sexuality* we participate in this process by practicing vulnerability, embracing our identity in Christ, and learning healthy intimacy. By growing in these three areas, we begin to display Christlike sexuality as sexual shame and sin lose their power.

This journey is not simply about avoiding sexual sin but about learning to love like Jesus. Through him, even in our sexually broken and battered world, freedom is real and healing is available. No matter what kind of sexual shame, sin, or brokenness you struggle with, there is good news for you: in Christ there is no condemnation (Romans 8:1), there is forgiveness and healing (1 Peter 2:24), and there is "everything we need for a godly life through our knowledge of him who called us by his own glory and goodness" (2 Peter 1:3). Though the journey of discipleship toward sexual wholeness is neither linear nor easy, change is possible because Christ is able. The only question left is: "Do you want to be healed?" (John 5:6 ESV).

GETTING THE MOST OUT OF
REDEEMED SEXUALITY

***Who is** Redeemed Sexuality *curriculum designed for?**

This curriculum is best used by small groups of four to eight people, between the ages of eighteen and thirty. It can be used by men or women in small groups separated by gender. Although both men and women experience sexual brokenness, they need to work through their issues in communities where potential love interests cannot get in the way. The priority of creating a safe space necessitates single-gender groups, due to the delicate and difficult nature of the subject matter.

What is the time commitment for participating in a group?

One ninety-minute small group time per week, plus at least one fifteen-minute prayer partner time per week.

This curriculum is designed for busy people, so aside from some preparation prior to session two, there are no required readings or tasks from session to session. However, in order to get the most out of the group, there is one requirement in addition to the weekly group meeting: between meetings, every par-ticipant needs to set up a regular time to connect with his or her prayer partner. It can be as short as five minutes or as long as an hour. It can be once a week or every night. It can happen over a meal or between classes. The point is to intentionally support one another during the week when we need it most, in times of trial, temptation, weakness, and struggle. Although the larger group will meet once each week for ninety minutes, it is imperative for members to connect in pairs or triads throughout the week.

In addition to the basic requirements of attending each weekly meeting and regularly connecting with your prayer partner(s), there are a number of ways to benefit from this curriculum more fully:

1. Journal through the journey. Journaling can have positive effects on your journey of sexual recovery, especially in developing self-awareness and intimacy with God. Journaling through *Redeemed Sexuality* helps you connect what you are learning to your own life. It helps you realize what is going well, what is going wrong, and how you can keep moving forward in the healing process. It can even be a form of prayer: of paying attention to what God is doing and talking with him about it. Each session includes a prompt for reflection at the end to help you start the conversation.

2. Find a sponsor. A sponsor is a person who is further along in the journey of healing and willing to mentor and coach you in ways that a peer prayer partner could not. In some cases, this person could be your group leader. In others, it could be a professor, a pastor, or an adult in your church. Spending time with a sponsor can encourage you, challenge you, and give you a picture of what it looks like to be a sexually and relationally healthy adult.

3. Read sexual recovery literature. If want to take your recovery to the next level, read what the experts have to say. You probably already have a lot of reading to do, especially if you're in school. But if you want a break from tedious textbooks, literature related to your group can serve as an exciting alternative! Ultimately, the more time and energy you invest in your healing and transformation, the more you will get out of this curriculum. If you're looking for a place to start, check out some of the recommended resources listed in the leader's notes.

Who can lead a group?

By design, this curriculum does not need to be led by experts or trained professionals. College students who are maturing in their journey of sexual recovery can use this book to lead a group of peers. This works especially well for students who are receiving support from a more experienced leader. Leaders do not have to be fully healed in order to lead a group; in fact, they need to be aware of their own continual need for healing and transformation. The best leaders are not those who are most impressive but who are most active in going through the process themselves, for their own benefit and the benefit of others.

Looking for tips and tools to help you lead weekly meetings? Check out the leader's notes for each session located in the back of the book.

How many weeks does it take to complete Redeemed Sexuality?

This curriculum is designed to be flexible and extendable. The twelve sessions can be completed either in one or two semesters. One-semester groups work for students who can't make a year-long commitment, while two-semester groups allow deeper relationships to form over time.

Each session takes up one ninety-minute weekly meeting (except session two), if you skip the Next Step material. The Next Step material is not meant to fit into weekly ninety-minute meetings. It can be completed outside of weekly meetings or take up an extra weekly meeting per session. This is what gives the curriculum the ability to double in length and last an entire school year (24 weeks).

What is the structure of a ninety-minute session?

Many groups decide to begin weekly meetings with a time for personal sharing. For a succinct yet effective structure to guide times of personal sharing, see appendix 1, "How to Check In."

◉ Welcome: An introduction to the week's session

  1. Review: A question building on the previous session.

2. Reframe: A transition from old content to new content.

3. Read: A passage of Scripture to read out loud together.

4. Request: A prayer for God's healing and transformation.

○ Main Activity: An experiential learning design intended to be completed in groups of two or three

1. After the prayer, the leader of the group will explain how the main activity works.

2. Then, everyone splits into their groups of two or three to complete the main activity together.

3. After everyone has finished the main activity, the leader then gathers everyone to regroup.

4. At this point, the group debriefs the main activity by talking together about how it went, what they learned, and how they can put what they learned into practice that week.

5. End the weekly meeting with a "closer" (for example, a song or the Lord's Prayer).

○ Next Step: An additional activity that does not fit into the ninety-minute weekly meeting. The Next Step activities offer more content for groups that want to focus on a specific area. Going through every Next Step activity would give your group enough content for an entire school year.

How should I use this book?

Redeemed Sexuality small group curriculum is not meant to be followed rigidly or programmatically. Mature small group leaders should feel free to depart from lesson plans in response to the specific needs of your group, as the Holy Spirit leads. It may be that your group needs to put the curriculum aside and simply spend an evening listening and praying for one another during a weekly meeting. That is perfectly fine! The goal is to grow in relationship with Christ and provide space for him to heal sexual brokenness. Whether you follow this curriculum word for word or simply use it as a resource to consult as you design your own meetings, remember: the point of these sessions is not to follow a formula but to create a community where we participate in the Holy Spirit's work of changing us to become more like the Son, as we experience the love of the Father.

The goal of *Redeemed Sexuality* is not to fix people or even to transform lives. God reserves that job for himself. Our goal is to create space for strong relationships to grow so healing can happen. True freedom from sexual shame and sin takes place in the context of relationships. Due to our relational nature as humans made in the image of God (Genesis 1:26-27), as well as the relational design of our sexuality (Genesis 2:18-25), we all need people who can truly see us, know us, and still love us.

Ultimately, when it comes to healing sexual brokenness, having group formulas is not as important as having good friends. That's why *Redeemed Sexuality* exists: to create the kind of communities where healing can happen.

Christ is the healer. He does not call us to fix people but to follow him. As Jesus said, "Apart from me you can do nothing" (John 15:5). So what do we actually do? Pursue intimacy with God and one another, and always be sensitive to the leading of the Holy Spirit. Persevere in prayer with the people in your group. Draw near to him whose touch heals the broken. It is Christ who brings sexual wholeness. We are simply joining him in what he is already doing.

FREQUENTLY ASKED QUESTIONS

Is Redeemed Sexuality *for people who identify as LGBTQ?*

This curriculum is for anyone who wants to find freedom and healing from sexual shame and sin. Those who experience same-sex attraction can benefit from joining a group just as much as those who do not. While *Redeemed Sexuality* addresses questions of identity in Christ, it does not answer questions about sexual identity based on arousal patterns.

How do you know when Redeemed Sexuality *might not be a good fit?*

Depending on the nature and severity of a person's sexual wounds, *Redeemed Sexuality* may not be a good fit. In cases of sexual abuse or severe addiction, counseling is a necessary part of recovery. *Redeemed Sexuality* is designed to serve as a guide for peer-led support groups; it cannot replace clinical treatment if it is needed.

Is Redeemed Sexuality *an alternative to receiving Christian counseling?*

Joining a group while meeting with a Christian counselor can be a powerful combination. The two serve different purposes and complement each other nicely. One-to-one counseling gives people in-depth guidance from an expert in the field, while groups give people the opportunity to heal and grow in community with other Christians going through the same thing. It is essentially a form of group therapy, which is often considered the gold standard of treatment. For some, *Redeemed Sexuality* is more than enough. For others, it will only be one piece of a larger process.

GROUP COVENANT

In order for a group to be a safe place where people can share deeply with one another, everyone who joins must agree to three nonnegotiable expectations.

COMMITMENT

I commit to prioritizing my sexual recovery by attending the ninety-minute group meeting every week.

I commit to connecting with my prayer partner(s) for one-on-one support at least once per week.

I commit to fully engaging in the disciplines that will lead to healing in my relationships with God, others, and myself. I commit to intentionally pursuing these goals with the members of my group.

I commit to participating fully in the activities of my group in a manner worthy of the gospel.

CONSISTENCY

I understand the need to attend every weekly meeting in order to fully benefit from this ministry.

I understand that each weekly meeting builds on the previous ones, and that missing a meeting will require help to catch up. I will do everything I can to stay in attendance as long as the group lasts.

CONFIDENTIALITY

I agree to keep all personal information shared in this group confidential within the group. I agree to receive all sexual confessions as private self-disclosure to intended listeners only. The only exception requiring me to break this rule would be a circumstance in need of intervention to prevent harm.

Respond to the invitation of Jesus: "Do you want to be healed?"
"Yes, I want to be healed. I desire sexual wholeness. I fully commit to this community."

Signed: _____

Name: _____ Phone Number: _____

VULNERABILITY

1

LEARNING THE LANGUAGE

God created sexuality to reveal Himself, how He operates,
and the value He places on intimate relating.

DOUGLAS ROSENAU, *A CELEBRATION OF SEX*

Welcome to *Redeemed Sexuality*! Well done—you have chosen the road to healing and transformation. Whether you have traveled this road for a long time or you are just starting the journey, this is an exciting and important step toward sexual health and freedom. This first session is a time to introduce ourselves to each other and set clear expectations for how this group will work.

REVIEW. Why did you decide to join this group?

REFRAME. We are all coming to this group from different places, with different experiences, and different ideas about sexuality: what it is, what it's for, and what healing could look like in our lives. This session introduces the basic language and concepts we'll use to talk about sexuality in this group, so that we can all start on the same page. But first, we'll remind ourselves of what we are committing to by joining this group.

READ. "Group Covenant" (p. 9).

REQUEST. Father of grace and healing, come heal our broken hearts and change our selfish ways. Make this group a safe place to talk about sexuality, where we can be supported and challenged to become more like your Son, Jesus, by the power of your Holy Spirit.

Note. Leaders, if you are prepared, share your sexual history at the end of this meeting (see fig. 1.1 on p. 20).

A COMMON VOCABULARY

The language we use to talk about sexual thoughts and behaviors makes a significant difference in the way we experience the healing process. Table 1.1 illustrates five different types of language we can use when talking about sexuality.

In a group, clinical language tends to be more helpful than slang or euphemism. For example, saying, "I watched pornography and

Table 1.1. Five types of sexual language

TYPE OF LANGUAGE	DEFINITION	EXAMPLES
clinical	anatomical words	intercourse, masturbation
slang	cultural words	getting laid, getting turned on
euphemism	vague words	doing it, making love
kiddie	childish words	"the birds and the bees"
poetic	symbolic words	Song of Solomon

Source: Christopher McCluskey and Rachel McCluskey, *When Two Become One: Enhancing Sexual Intimacy in Marriage* (Grand Rapids: Revell, 2004), 39-41.

masturbated twice" communicates more clearly and descriptively than saying, "I messed up" or "I fell." Vague euphemisms like "I fell" can be used as walls to hide behind. We want to use nonjudgmental language that is specific enough to be clear while avoiding crude, immature, or inappropriate descriptions of sexual thoughts and behaviors. It is also possible to be *too* specific and give so much information that it can cause others to stumble. So although we don't need to shy away from using explicit sexual language, we don't need to dwell on it either. Because there is no single type of language that works in all circumstances, we must use discernment to choose which language to use in a given situation. Since clinical language is most often the appropriate type of language to use in a group, everyone in your group should become familiar with important technical sexual terms relating to sexuality, sexual brokenness, and sexual wholeness.

This section is intended to give you a shared vocabulary of sexual language to use in your group. It is not a comprehensive list but a tool to promote healthy dialogue. Learning to think and talk about sexuality differently starts with a clear understanding of terminology.

- Scan through the terms on pages 14-17.

- What questions do you have about any of these terms?

Sexuality is our God-given capacity for intimate relating and connecting. Sexuality is a much larger category than sex. It describes who we are as human beings. We are sexual at our core, whether or not we participate in sexual behaviors. All human relationships involve sexuality in some way, because sexuality affects all of life. Sexuality is an integral part of how our relational God created us in his image as male and female, to live in close relationships with him and one other.

The following list describes several aspects of our sexuality. Although these aspects may be difficult to control, they are not innately sinful—instead, they are opportunities for us to glorify God with our bodies (1 Corinthians 6:20).

- *Sexual desires* are longings for intimate connection, designed to draw us closer to God and others.

- *Sexual surges* are periods of especially strong sexual desire, "feeling horny." This is normal and good.

- *Sexual aches* are deep undercurrents of longing for romance and relationship. This is also normal and good.

- *Sexual temptation* is the desire to pursue sexual satisfaction in a way contrary to

God's design. Sexual temptation itself is not sinful (Hebrews 4:15); it only becomes sinful when we decide to give in to it.

- *Sexual pleasure* includes positive experiences of sexual stimulation meant to enhance loving relationships.

- *Sexual union* is full sexual exposure and contact shared between two people—what most people call "having sex."

- *Same-sex attraction* is when an individual is attracted to those of the same gender. It is helpful to note the distinction between attraction and behavior.

Sexual brokenness is what happens when sexuality is used for selfish gain rather than self-giving love. Sometimes this brokenness is the result of what we have done; sometimes it is the result of what others have done to us. Sexual brokenness can be both a cause and an effect of deep wounds and broken relationships, changing God's good gift of sexuality into a burden rather than a blessing. It is essentially a form of relational impoverishment, including spiritual, social, mental, emotional, biological, and systemic dimensions.

Sexual brokenness includes the following terms:

- *Sexual sin* is any attitude or action that departs from or rebels against God's design for sexuality.

- *Sexual lust* is the sin of focusing on someone as an object of your sexual desire for selfish purposes. Love gives; lust takes.

- *Sexual shame* is self-loathing and condemnation rooted in sexual issues. Sexual shame is different from sexual guilt. It has been said that we experience guilt when we know we have made a mistake (which is often true), but we experience shame when we believe we are a mistake (which is a lie from the enemy).

- *Sexual harassment* is "unwelcome conduct of a sexual nature, including unwelcome sexual advances, requests for sexual favors, and other verbal, nonverbal, graphic, or physical conduct of a sexual nature, without regard to whether the parties are of the same or different genders."

- *Sexual assault* is "a particular type of sexual harassment that includes physical sexual acts perpetrated when consent is not present, where a person is incapable of giving consent, or coercion and/or force is used. This includes nonconsensual sexual contact, as well as nonconsensual sexual intercourse or penetration."

- *Sexual abuse* is anything that hinders and inhibits healthy sexual development, including but not limited to traumatic sexual experiences. Under this definition, sexual abuse can be physical, verbal, emotional, or spiritual: anything that has hindered our sexual development. Sexual abuse often comes from parents, pastors, or peers who may or may not have intended to hurt us. Sexual abuse is the always fault of the sexual abuser, not the sexually abused.

- *Sexual addiction* refers to an unhealthy pattern of sexual behavior that has become unmanageable. The pattern continues to escalate despite increasing negative consequences to one's self or others. Sexual addiction is a condition of the brain. Sexually addicted people have trained their brains to seek out sexual stimulation as a mood-altering experience rather than a way to connect with others. For the addict, sexual activity functions as a coping mechanism to medicate underlying pain.

○ *Sexual co-addiction (or codependency)* refers to an unhealthy pattern of compromising one's own sexual values in order to avoid rejection. Partners of sexual addicts are people who enable others to engage in unwelcome sexual activity. They may allow a partner or spouse to mistreat them or to cheat on them with someone else. They will ignore the problem, rejecting their own feelings as invalid and seeking validation from another person. *They too require sexual recovery.*

○ *Sexual strongholds* are power bases of sexual thoughts, lies, and habits standing in opposition to Christ.

○ *Sexual indulgence* is giving in to sexual temptation via sinful behavior; also known as "acting out."

○ *Sexual repression* is the willful suppression and suffocation of sexual desire, also known as "acting in."

○ *Sexual accusation* is the voice of condemnation and self-loathing in response to sexual sin and shame.

○ *Slips* are one-time, isolated instances of briefly returning into sexually broken behaviors before admitting it and recommitting to recovery. SLIP = Short Lapse in Progress.

○ *Relapses* are periods of repeated returns into sexually broken behaviors. In a relapse the person acts out, but chooses not to admit or address it, and abandons the road to recovery.

○ *Masturbation* refers to sexual self-stimulation culminating in orgasm, often paired with pornography use, but not necessarily. "Masturbation teaches us that immediate gratification is a part of sex, and masturbation removes sex from a relationship. Indeed, the whole point of masturbation is to provide the release and pleasure of orgasm without the work and joy of a relationship."

○ *Pornography* refers to the graphic depiction of human bodies in order to elicit sexual arousal. However, different kinds of media can be used pornographically even if they were not intended to produce such an effect. It must also be noted that pornography is not only an issue of private morality but of systematic injustice. The 100 billion-dollar industry of Internet pornography perpetuates sex trafficking around the world.

Sexual wholeness is what happens when sexuality fulfills God's design as a vehicle for self-giving love. Sexual wholeness can be both a cause and an effect of healing relationships with God and others. Sexually healthy people experience God's good gift of sexuality not as a burden but as a blessing that draws them out of themselves into life as it was meant to be lived. Sexual health is a form of relational flourishing that includes spiritual, relational, mental, emotional, biological, and systemic dimensions. Sexually whole people worship God by enjoying life and loving others with abandon!

Sexual wholeness includes the following terms.

○ *Sexual purity* is the state of living in complete harmony with God's design for human sexuality.

○ *Sexual integrity* is the practice of behaving in complete harmony with one's own sexual standards.

○ *Sexual discipline* is the practice of continually

reforming one's sexual desires, thoughts, and actions.

○ *Sexual discipleship* is the process of becoming more and more Christlike in regard to our sexuality.

○ *Sexual freedom* is the experience of regaining independence from unwanted, unmanageable sexual patterns.

○ *Sexual healing (or sexual recovery)* is the process of regaining sexual wholeness for those who have experienced sexual shame, sin, addiction, assault, or abuse.

○ *Sexual sobriety (or being sexually sober)* is a state in which someone going through sexual recovery successfully refrains from unhealthy or addictive behaviors.

Sexual contexts are the life situations in which we are called to steward our sexuality. Not all of us find ourselves in the same situation, sexually speaking. While we are all called to the same set of standards according to God's design for sexuality, the way we are called to live out those standards depends on the sexual context we find ourselves inhabiting. Appropriate sexual contexts include the following possibilities:

○ *Singleness* is being uncoupled, a context in which sexual desires are to be directed nonerotically.

○ *Celibacy* is a commitment to abstain from marriage/sexual union for the sake of God's kingdom.

○ *Dating* is a middle ground for couples to learn, grow, and discern between singleness and marriage.

○ *Marriage* is a covenant of lifelong sexual monogamy between a man and a woman, made before God and the surrounding community. Marriage is the only appropriate context for sexual union according to God's design.

NEXT STEP: PREPARING YOUR STORY

This week, your leader has shared his or her story with you. The following exercise will prepare you for the next time you gather, when all other members will share their stories. (Note: This is the only required "homework assignment" you will ever have for this group—and it must be completed before the next gathering.)

Telling your story is never easy, but it's the first step to finding freedom and healing from sexual brokenness. It involves talking about parts of your life that are painful, ugly, and shame-filled. Telling your story well requires taking a long, hard look into your own past and present before bringing the darkness into the light when you share with your group.

This will require ruthless honesty. Whatever shameful experience you might be hesitant about sharing is exactly what you need to share. It is *so* vulnerable, *so* scary, *so* necessary, and *so* freeing. When you unload your heaviest baggage, even the things that make you disgusted with yourself, the response will not be scorn. The response will be relief as people realize that they are not the only ones who hurt. There, the place of deep rejection and self-loathing becomes the place of deep grace and acceptance. The next pages will help you process your own story individually before sharing it with the group the next time you meet.

1. Scan through the two boxes of table 1.2 below and circle any words (positive or negative) that have played an important part in your sexual history.

Table 1.2. Sexuality history terms

POSITIVE EXPERIENCES		NEGATIVE EXPERIENCES	
acceptance	identity	abandonment	helplessness
beauty	integrity	abuse	hiding
belonging	intimacy	alienation	hopelessness
character	joy	anger	inadequacy
clarity	leadership	angst	insecurity
community	love	anxiety	lack of sleep
compassion	peace	apathy	lies
confession	prayer	arrogance	loneliness
confidence	purity	bitterness	lust
connection	purpose	boredom	numbness
contentment	responsibility	cheating	objectification
delight	righteousness	comparison	pressure
deliverance	sanctification	consumerism	pride
dignity	satisfaction	control	regret
discipleship	security	denial	rejection
faithfulness	selflessness	depression	self-absorption
forgiveness	service	despair	self-loathing
freedom	strength	disappointment	self-righteousness
friendship	surrender	doubt	shame
grace	transformation	emptiness	slumps
gratitude	trust	entitlement	stagnation
growth	truth	envy	temptation
healing	vulnerability	exhaustion	unbelief
holiness	wholeness	fear	unforgiveness
honesty	worship	gluttony	victimization
hope		greed	violence
		guilt	workaholism
		hatred	

2. Explore the "Sexuality concept bank" (table 1.3) and recall any significant elements, events, people, or places that shaped your sexuality. Note any especially emotional memories.

3. Fill in the following lines with key points you will share when you tell your story.

Something I definitely want to share with my group: _____

Something God has already done that I want to share: _____

Something I still need help with that I want to share: _____

Something I am afraid to share with my group: _____

4. Trace a timeline of your sexual history (see fig. 1.1 on p. 20), using elements from the "Sexuality concept bank" as well as other important experiences and turning points related to your sexuality.

Table 1.3. Sexuality concept bank

relationship with mother	undesired sexual experiences	unmet expectations
relationship with siblings	experiences of same-sex attraction	my view of God
parents' ideas about sexuality	hurtful words said to me	my view of myself
parents' silence about sexuality	encouraging words said to me	my view of women
church's ideas about sexuality	positive role models/heroes	my view of men
culture's ideas about sexuality	negative role models/enemies	turning points in my life
TV shows, movies, books, media	people who rejected me	experiences of growth
messages about body image	people who accepted me	experiences of relapse
messages about singleness	groups I was a part of	times I kept secrets
messages about marriage	first orgasm	times I was confronted
messages about dating	masturbation	times I opened up to others
grade school crushes	pornography	success in resisting temptation
middle school crushes	objectification	failure in resisting temptation
middle school friendships	sexual fantasies	circumstances in which I'm most
high school friendships	experiments with sex acts	susceptible to temptation
high school crushes	what I find sexually attractive	realization that I have a problem
dating experiences	what I find attractive in friends	hopes for how I will change
healthy levels of intimacy	dreams of romance	fears for what will come next
unhealthy levels of intimacy	deep-seated desires	my decision to join this group
desired sexual experiences	expectations for love	

Sexual struggles cannot be properly understood apart from the events and experiences they emerged from. Henri Nouwen encourages us to come face-to-face with the difficult and dark parts of our stories so that they no longer keep us from experiencing true healing in the present:

> Forgetting the past is like turning our most intimate teacher against us. By refusing to face our painful memories we miss the opportunity to change our hearts and grow mature in repentance. When Jesus says, "It is not the healthy who need the doctor, but the sick" (Mark 2:17) He affirms that only those who face their wounded condition can be available for healing and so enter into a new way of living. . . . How are we healed of our wounding memories? We are healed first of all by letting them be available, by leading them out of the corner of forgetfulness and by remembering them as part of our life stories. What is forgotten is unavailable, and what is unavailable cannot be healed.
>
> Henri Nouwen, *The Living Reminder*

Figure 1.1. My sexual history

REFLECTION

Taking a moment to reflect can be a powerful part of this experience (see appendix 3).

After each session, there will be space for you to reflect on your experiences in this group. Each space for reflection will include prompts like the following questions to help you get started.

What hopes do you have for this group?

What fears do you have for this group?

2

TELLING YOUR STORY

*If we can share our story with someone who responds with
empathy and understanding, shame can't survive.*

BRENÉ BROWN, *DARING GREATLY*

Why do we jump into sharing our sexual histories right away? Because it sets the tone for the rest of our time together. Trust is built and safety is established. People will talk more openly about sexual struggles after experiencing the power of bringing their darkness into the light. Once everyone has disclosed their sexual histories, the group becomes a place of acceptance and authentic community. People experience God's grace through one another, and prayer partners are able to offer each other day-to-day support at a deeper level. Telling our stories is usually scary, but always worth it.

REVIEW. How do you feel about sharing your sexual history?

REFRAME. Sharing our sexual histories is one way to obey James 5:16, which instructs us to pursue healing by confessing our sins and praying for one another. While it would be interesting to do an in-depth study of verses like James 5:16, the focus of this group is not on studying the Bible but putting what it says into practice. This session introduces the practices of confession and prayer. It is not meant to be a one-time event, but the first step in developing a habit of talking about these things regularly. The "next step" will give you guidelines for organizing prayer partners so that person-to-person confession and prayer become life-giving habits.

READ. James 5:16.

Therefore confess your sins to each other and
pray for each other so that you may be healed.
The prayer of a righteous person is powerful
and effective.

REQUEST. Holy Spirit, make us brave. We need courage to be honest about what we have done and about what has been done to us. Jesus, help us to see our stories through your eyes, to see how you have been at work this whole time to heal and restore our sexually broken lives. Help us to listen to one another with love and to accept one another as you have accepted us. Amen.

SHARING STORIES

Stories take time. Telling everyone's stories is the one activity in *Redeemed Sexuality* that takes longer than ninety minutes. The best strategy is to gather for a few hours on the weekend for all to share their stories. If your group is not able to carve out any space on the weekend, you can do it in two weekly meetings if you set aside more time than normal (see table 2.1).

Order of telling stories:

○ Set a timer for twenty-five minutes as a guideline for how long to talk.

○ Leave time at the end of each story for people to ask follow-up questions.

○ Invite two people to pray for each person after the story has been told.

○ Take a five minute rest period after every story.

Hopefully, hearing everyone's stories will help your group decide who would work well together as prayer partners. Whether it's during a weekly meeting or not, be sure to organize prayer partners so that story sharing does not become a one-time emotional release but an ongoing conversation. Once you do this, you can support one another more effectively throughout the week!

Table 2.1. Time needed for sharing stories

ESTIMATED TIME NEEDED PER STORY		
Telling one person's story	25-30 minutes	
Time for follow-up questions	5 minutes	
Two people pray for the person	5 minutes	
Total time needed for each person	35-40 minutes	
ESTIMATED TIME NEEDED PER GROUP		
	One night	*Two nights*
Group size: 3-4	2-3 hours	1-2 hours each
Group size: 5-6	4-5 hours	2-3 hours each
Group size: 7-8	5-6 hours	3-4 hours each

NEXT STEP: PRAYER PARTNERS

Arrange your group into prayer partners: smaller units of two or three. These partnerships are not only for prayer but for confession, affirmation, personal challenge, and spiritual friendship. The goal is not accountability in the sense of sexually policing one another by keeping tabs on bad behaviors, but ministering the gospel to one another when we need it most. Weekly group meetings alone cannot accomplish this. Daily contact with your prayer partner(s) is where the main action of discipleship happens, not in weekly group meetings.

Attending weekly meetings is a good place to start. However, if you don't connect with a prayer partner at least once per week outside of group meetings, you will seriously stunt your ability to grow. There are at least two major reasons for this: First, sexual shame and sin is not a once-a-week problem, so discipleship in this area cannot succeed as a once-a-week solution. Second, sexual shame and sin is ultimately an *intimacy disorder* that feeds on silence and isolation, so healing

Perhaps the most important skill to learn in *Redeemed Sexuality* is relying on one another in the body of Christ rather than relying on ourselves. That's what prayer partners are for. Adele Ahlberg Calhoun unpacks the amazing potential of what can happen through these relationships:

> Accountability partners help us face into the truth of who we are in Christ. They help us face down the lies that shape us, and they orient us in the direction of God's patient love. Together, accountability partners walk into the temptations and difficulties of life. They share the last 10 percent of themselves with each other. They let their secrets out. And together they focus on living holy and responsible lives, fueled by desire for God. Regular and prayerful companionship becomes a life-changing vehicle of God's grace.
>
> Adele Ahlberg Calhoun, *Spiritual Disciplines Handbook*

requires you to replace silence with consistent communication and replace isolation by spending time together with someone who can support you.

Time with your prayer partner does not have to be long; even fifteen minutes is usually enough. The key is consistency. The most successful prayer partners connect frequently, if not nightly. By doing so, they support one another not only in response to problems but by preventing problems before they happen. Prayer partners minister to one another in the ugliness and messiness of daily problems. No amount of *trying* to heal on your own can substitute for the *training* you do with a prayer partner.

Think of your group as a team. The weekly meeting is your team's huddle.

The huddle is where you prepare for game time, when trials and temptations come. Even if the huddle goes well, if you don't play as a team during game time, you will be easily defeated. The opponent's strategy is to divide and conquer, because if you try to fight sexual shame and sin alone, you will soon grow discouraged. However, if you play as a team, you will be difficult to defeat. Prayer partners help us to play as a team during game time, not just during the huddle.

PRAYING TOGETHER CAN HEAL OUR WHOLE LIVES, INCLUDING OUR...

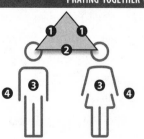

1. **Relationship with God:** spiritual intimacy and safety *recovered* and *restored*

2. **Relationship with others:** quality of personal closeness and connection *renewed*

3. **Relationship with self:** vision of identity as a beloved son or daughter of God *regained*

4. **Relationship with world:** freedom to thrive in other positive occupations *released*

Figure 2.1. Prayer partners

WHAT TO DO WITH YOUR PRAYER PARTNER

- Pray together at least once per week.
- Call for help during trials and temptations.
- Always be honest about struggles and sins.
- Answer the phone when called for help.
- Explore areas of woundedness.
- Encourage often and challenge with truth.
- Notice and affirm signs of improvement.
- Clarify the boundaries of the friendship.

QUESTIONS FOR PRAYER PARTNERS

What is the best time for us to get together between meetings?

What days and times are we each most likely to need help?

What days and times will we be unavailable to talk and pray?

Who will we call for help if the other person is unavailable?

What else would be helpful for us to know about each other?

TIP FOR PRAYER PARTNERS: DOWNLOAD AND USE THE "RTRIBE" APP TO STAY CONNECTED.

REFLECTION

What was it like for you to share your sexual history with your group?

What was one part of your story or someone else's story that stood out to you?

3

WOUNDS OF THE PAST

✳————————————————————————————————————◄◄◄◄

*Sexual addiction and sexual bondage are not so much
about sex as about coping with the pain within.*

TED ROBERTS, *PURE DESIRE*

Last session you told your story. This required incredible courage and vulnerability to share intimate information with the members of your group. The next step is to *process* your story, to deal with the past so that you can move forward in the present. Often, we don't process wounds we received in the past, either because we are unaware of them or unwilling to face them. Yet if we look beneath our sexual struggles, we will discover that they are related to painful experiences from our past. We turn to sexual stimulation to cope with events and emotions we would rather not think about. We wish we could make the pain go away, and (without realizing it) use sexual activity to fill the void.

So before we address unwanted sexual behaviors, first we need to process the unresolved wounds behind them. This is hard work, especially after doing the heavy lifting of telling your story. Take heart! Your group is becoming a safe place where you can be supported and strengthened as you engage in the healing process. Taking this journey *together* can help you feel more motivated to make peace with the parts of your sexual history that you wish would not have happened. It is normal to feel hesitant about this. Allow the Lord to reveal any new insights, as painful and difficult as they may be, as you take a deeper look into the wounds of your past.

REVIEW. In your story, what events and experiences were most difficult for you?

REFRAME. In order to deal with pain from our past, forgiveness is a necessary part of the healing journey. This session invites you to begin the process of forgiving those who have hurt you and negatively affected your sexuality. Like telling your story, forgiveness is not a one-time event but an ongoing journey. You may need to forgive the same person for the same thing again and again. It may be that you are not yet ready to forgive. If this is you, give yourself time to grieve what happened to you and simply recognize how others have hurt you. Especially if you have experienced sexual assault or abuse, you may want to skip or postpone this exercise because it reopens old wounds in need of great attention. While your small group can provide a safe space for these things to surface, it would be wise to speak to a counselor for deeper processing and healing.

READ. Ephesians 4:31-32.

> Get rid of all bitterness, rage and anger, brawling and slander, along with every form of malice. Be kind and compassionate to one another, forgiving each other, just as in Christ God forgave you.

REQUEST. Jesus, we need your power to forgive the sins of those who have harmed us, just as you forgave us for harming you. We are wounded by pain we did not deserve, and by love we did not receive. Send your Spirit to minister to us, so that we may rest in the love of the Father. Amen.

FORGIVENESS

This exercise invites you to take a step toward forgiving those who have contributed to your sexual brokenness. It's best done in pairs, which creates an intimate setting where everyone gets to speak and feel heard in a way they would not be able to in the larger group. It also allows for enough time and space to say the prayer of forgiveness out loud for each person on your list. This strategy of splitting into pairs for personal sharing is a great way to approach many of the other exercises as well.

Ultimately, forgiveness is not a feeling, but a choice. It is a willful act to stop harboring re-

sentment or ill will toward another person. For some hurts, you may need to repeatedly forgive whenever the person who hurt you comes to mind. Forgiveness is a crucial part of the healing process. Although you might not realize it, hidden bitterness can keep you trapped in sexual bondage.

You may also need to forgive yourself. As Neil T. Anderson writes, "Forgiving yourself is accepting the truth that God has already forgiven you in Christ." You don't need to continue living in shame over your sins and imperfections. You can acknowledge that despite what you've done, what Jesus has done for you is far greater. If you need to forgive yourself, include your name in table 3.1.

By the end of this exercise, you will probably feel emotionally exhausted. If you do end up taking a step toward forgiving those who have hurt you, remember that this is evidence of the Holy Spirit's work in your life, transforming you to become more like Jesus.

1. Ask the Lord to bring to mind any especially painful parts of your story.

2. Think of any people you can forgive for the way they hurt or hindered you (for example, things that were said to you or done to you, rejections, unhealthy relationships, bad breakups, family trauma, scarring experiences).

3. Pray the following prayer according to the instructions. (*Note:* This prayer is to be spoken to God, not to the offender.)

> Lord, I know I need to forgive [name the person] for [say what they did to hurt you] even though it made me feel [share the painful feelings]. I confess that when [name the person] did this, I reacted by [identify how you reacted].

Table 3.1. List of wounds of the past

PERSON WHO HURT ME	WHAT THIS PERSON DID	HOW IT MADE ME FEEL	SINFUL REACTIONS I MAY HAVE HAD

If you're not quite ready to forgive the person who hurt you, then stop here. However, if you are ready to forgive, then also pray:

In this moment, I repent and choose to stop holding these things against [name the person] any longer. Instead, I choose to forgive [name the person], just as you have forgiven me. I ask you to bless [name the person] in the name of Jesus. Amen.

As you go through this process, you may also recognize your need to ask for forgiveness of others. Although this is often a very healthy response, sometimes we need to seek wise counsel from a pastor, small group leader, or trusted friend to walk alongside us as we seek forgiveness or even reconciliation.

You may or may not feel a sense of closure after completing this session, and that's okay. This exercise is meant to initiate a process of healing old wounds that will continue long after your group ends. For the rest of our lives, we will continue to discover the ways our experiences have shaped us, good and bad, and ways we need to receive God's healing love.

NEXT STEP: FAMILY ISSUES

We are often unaware of how our family relationships affect our sexuality. The families we grew up in taught us how to be a girl or a boy, a woman or a man, and what it means to be a sexual human being. Even though not all of our families talked openly about sex, even their silence or avoidance of the topic was communicating and teaching us something. For some of us, when it came to sexuality, our families taught us what we should avoid more than what we should pursue. Our families also taught us how to love and be loved.

Sexual brokenness is so much deeper than what we see on the surface. To deal with it, we not only need to examine what we've done but what has been done to us. This is not fun, but as Mark Laaser explains, it is a necessary part of the healing process:

> It is important for sexual addicts to recognize that their sexual activity is an attempt to medicate old wounds and to find love. To begin, they must understand what their wounds are. Understanding wounds leads addicts back to the dynamics involved in their families. Understanding these dynamics begins the process of healing. Sexual addicts who are in recovery from their disease do not blame family members for their addiction. They also do not seek to avoid their own responsibility for getting well. Recovering addicts, however, must understand what happened to them and understand that they didn't deserve them. They must admit they did not receive the love and nurturing they needed, and that many of the messages they learned have been wrong. Understanding these things is crucial to changing opinions of themselves and others. It is also crucial in finding the love and nurturing they never got but always wanted.
>
> Mark Laaser, *Healing the Wounds of Sexual Addiction*

The following exercise gives you an opportunity to explore how your family of origin shaped your view of sexuality and relationships. The purpose is not to pass blame onto our families, nor to deflect responsibility for our own actions, but to develop greater self-awareness.

1. In the table below, circle any statements describing attitudes toward sexuality your family taught you.

Table 3.2. Family messages about sexuality

"Your sexuality is about whatever makes you happy."	"Sex? We don't talk about that."
"Sexuality is a beautiful part of how God made us."	"Marriage will satisfy your sexual desires."
"If you stay sexually pure, God will bless you."	"Sexual sins are worse than other sins."
"Being single is just as good as being married."	"One day God will give you a spouse."
"Do what you want, just don't hurt anyone."	"If you've had sex, you're damaged goods."
"Sex is so much better when you wait."	"Sex is meant to be celebrated and protected."
"Sexuality is basically about having sex."	"Pornography is dangerous and destructive."
"Sexual attraction is normal and good."	"Sexuality is private, not for public conversation."
"Your body is a temple of the Holy Spirit."	"Somewhere out there, 'The One' is waiting for you."
"Don't think about sex until you're married."	"Sexual pleasure is the highest form of pleasure."
"You'll figure it out when you get older."	"Sexuality is meant to be an expression of God's love."

Add one of your own:

2. Consider how these messages have affected your sexual behavior. Which ones influenced you the most?

We did not only learn from what our families said (or didn't say) about sex, but by what they did and how they treated us. We need to realize how our families hurt or hindered our sexual development. These are deep waters. If you realize the need to process your past more fully, consider seeing a professional counselor or therapist to explore these issues in more depth.

3. Using the table below, identify how your family members related to you in positive and negative ways.

Table 3.3. Family actions

FAMILY MEMBER	LOVING ACTIONS	UNLOVING ACTIONS
For example: my sibling	spent quality time with me	verbally put me down

How have your parents affected the way you relate to the opposite sex?

How have your siblings affected the way you relate to the opposite sex?

How might your sexual struggles be an attempt to get the love you wanted but never received?

REFLECTION

What connections did you see between your wounds of the past and your current sexual struggles?

How can you continue to embrace a healthier approach to sexuality than the one you grew up with?

4

TRUTH AND LIES

What are the specific lies your sinful desires tell you? Identify them and then go to God's word and find passages that specifically address those lies.

JOSHUA HARRIS, *SEX IS NOT THE PROBLEM (LUST IS)*

The first two sessions were about dealing with the past; this session is about understanding our struggles in the present. We will use a real-life case study as a starting point to talk about the deep-seated realities underneath sexual brokenness. You'll learn how to name triggers, feelings, fears, and lies beneath the surface of sexual sin and shame: first in the case study, and then in your own life.

REVIEW. At what point do our sexual desires become sinful? (See Matthew 5:27-28; James 1:13-15.)

REFRAME. Too often, people try to stop sexual behaviors without ever realizing or addressing the deeper issues going on in their hearts and minds. They don't see that the sexual surface symptoms they are dealing with are part of a bigger problem. Sexual thoughts and desires are not the problem; in fact, they are good gifts created by God. The bigger problem behind sexual brokenness has to do with starved relationships, destructive thought patterns, disordered desires, and unhealthy ways of dealing with emotions. The goal is not to get rid of our sexual desires but to understand them and

respond to them in ways that are healthy and holy. Solely telling ourselves the truth and trying harder is inadequate; we have to identify the lies behind the scenes of sexual shame and sin.

READ. Psalm 51:1-2, 10.

Have mercy on me, O God,
　　according to your unfailing love;
according to your great compassion
　　blot out my transgressions.
Wash away all my iniquity
　　and cleanse me from my sin. . . .

Create in me a pure heart, O God,
　　and renew a steadfast spirit within me.

REQUEST. God, you created our sexuality and called it good. But we took it into our own hands for selfish purposes. We have rejected your love and listened to lies; we need you to rewire our brains and replace our lust with your love. Wash us by your Word and renew our minds with truth. Amen.

LEAVES AND ROOTS

With your group, read the case study and see what thought patterns you can notice. (Note: If you are in a women's group, read "Ashley's Story." If you are in a men's group, read "Tom's Story.")

Begin by identifying surface triggers and feelings (the leaves), and then underlying fears and lies (the roots) (see fig. 4.1).

1. Talk about events that triggered Ashley or Tom.

2. Notice as many triggers as you can. (Use the "Triggers" box.)

3. Describe how those triggers must have made Ashley or Tom feel. (Use the "Feelings" box.)

4. Name the difficult or painful emotions he or she is trying to cope with. (Only after making a list of triggers and feelings will you be ready to uncover the fears and lies that are controlling the person's thought life.)

5. Offer your perspective on this question: "What is this person is *really* afraid of, deep down?" (Use the "Fears" box.)

6. Name any lies that might be at the root of those fears. (Use the "Lies" box.)

7. What truths do you think Ashley or Tom especially needs to hear?

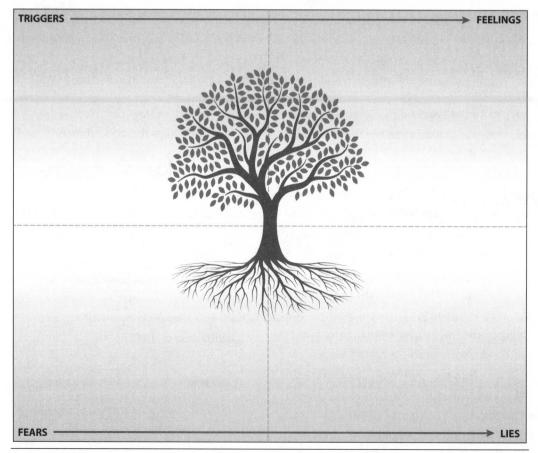

Figure 4.1. Leaves and roots

ASHLEY'S STORY

Consider the following example of Ashley, a single woman in her twenties who had significant problems with pornography and masturbation. After viewing pornography and sexually acting out, she wrote in her journal and reviewed the previous twenty-four hours.

1. Last night I was up late working on a group project. I went to bed around 3 a.m.

2. I got up on time for class, but was tired.

3. My part of the project was not well received by our professor at our 9 a.m. class.

4. I kept working on the project with my group for the rest of the morning. I felt useless.

5. The transfer student in our group smiled at me when I made a joke about his man bun.

6. I found myself fantasizing about him, even though I knew I wasn't genuinely interested.

7. I wanted to talk to him again, so I made up a reason to go over and ask him for help and started flirting with him. I hadn't ever thought of him in a romantic way before, but that morning I toyed with the idea a little.

8. My professor walked by while I was flirting and let me know that my lack of participation was bringing down my group's final grade.

9. I was embarrassed and knew the transfer student would never be attracted to me or want to go out with me.

10. I sank back into my seat and fumed about my professor. I wanted to drop the class or find a way to get back at him.

11. My group went to lunch at the cafeteria, but I made up an excuse to go back to my apartment. I closed the blinds on my windows and locked the door to my room. I thought viewing porn would be a good way to feel better and de-stress.

12. Viewing the pictures on my phone aroused me, and I really felt the need to masturbate.

13. I viewed the pictures until someone knocked on the door. The images on my phone seemed to take forever to disappear.

14. It was my roommate. She asked why the door was locked and was suspicious of what I was doing. I told her I was still working on the project. She told me she didn't know what was going on but felt like I was hiding something.

15. I realized I was perspiring excessively and my hair was messy. I felt like I had narrowly avoided being caught.

16. I was preoccupied with my fixing my hair for the rest of the afternoon.

17. I met up with the group again to finish our project. When I saw the transfer student laughing with another girl about something that happened at lunch, I felt a pang. I tried to be extra friendly as we worked, but he seemed disinterested. My hair was a mess and I felt unattractive.

18. I thought about him the entire walk home. I passed another male friend and he smiled at me.

19. My roommate wasn't home and had left a note saying she would be gone for the weekend.

20. While changing out of my clothes, I took a few moments to admire myself in the mirror. I couldn't help but wonder how a guy would feel if he saw me naked. I undressed, closed the blinds to the windows, collapsed into bed, and got out my phone. I knew I was going to view porn and I didn't care.

21. I looked for hardcore images of men with long hair for about ten minutes. (I knew right where to go because I've been there before.) I found a video clip of a male model that looked like the transfer student.

22. I looped the video for a couple of minutes, masturbating to it.

23. I felt even sweatier and messier when I was done, so I took a shower.

24. I felt worthless and trapped. I was disgusted with myself.

TOM'S STORY

Consider the following example of Tom. Tom is a single man in his twenties who had significant problems with pornography and masturbation. After viewing pornography and sexually acting out, he wrote in his journal and reviewed the previous twenty-four hours.

1. Last night I was up late working on a project for work. I went to bed around 3 a.m.

2. I got up on time for work, but was tired.

3. My project was not well received by my boss at our 9 a.m. meeting.

4. I avoided my boss the rest of the morning. Avoiding him put me on edge.

5. The new woman in accounting smiled at me when she dropped off a report.

6. I found myself fantasizing about her, and I got an erection.

7. I wanted to see her again, so I made up a reason to stop at her office and started flirting with her.

8. My boss walked by while I was flirting and ripped into me about the project again.

9. I was embarrassed and knew she would never be attracted to me or want to have sex with me.

10. I went back to my desk and fumed about my boss. I wanted to quit or find a way to get back at him.

11. Everyone left the office for a working lunch, but I made up an excuse to stay behind. I closed the blinds on my windows and locked the office door. I thought viewing porn would be a good way to get back at my boss.

12. Viewing the pictures gave me an erection, and I really felt the need to masturbate.

13. I viewed the pictures until someone knocked on the door. The images on the screen seemed to take forever to disappear.

14. It was my boss. He asked why the door was locked and was suspicious of what I was doing. I told him I was working on revisions to the report. He told me the next report had better be up to his standards.

15. I realized I was perspiring excessively and thought I smelled of sex. I felt like I had narrowly avoided being caught and erased the files from my computer.

16. I was preoccupied with my body odor for the rest of the afternoon.

17. The new woman from accounting brought the new report back right before 5 p.m. I reeked of sweat and was sure she could smell it.

18. I fantasized about her the entire drive home and had an erection.

19. My roommate wasn't home and had left a note saying he would be gone for the weekend.

20. While changing from my work clothes I was reminded of my body odor, the smell of sex, again. I undressed, closed the blinds to the windows, got some tissue paper, and then went online. I knew I was going to view porn and I didn't care.

21. I surfed for hardcore images of secretaries for about ten minutes. (I knew right where to go because I've been there before.) I found a video clip of a secretary that looked like the new accountant.

22. I looped the video for a couple of minutes, masturbating to it.

23. I smelled even more of sweat when I was done, so I took a shower.

24. I felt miserable and trapped. I was disgusted with myself.

YOUR TURN

On your own, recall the most recent situation when you faced sexual temptation, sin, or shame. Analyze it the way you analyzed the case study by filling out the figure below. Then process it with one or two other people.

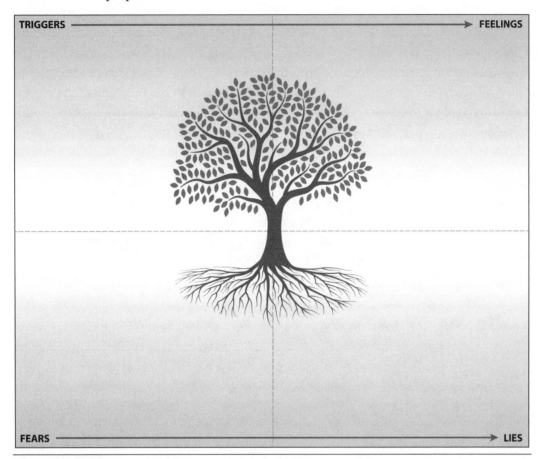

Figure 4.2. Your turn

NEXT STEP: MEMORIZATION

Think back to Ashley's or Tom's case study and your own. Look at the lies that lurked at the roots of our sexually broken behaviors. In those moments, what truths needed to be spoken? Counteract the lies of the enemy by filling our minds with truth from God's Word. The psalmist seems especially aware of how necessary this is for us when he asks, "How can a young person stay on the path of purity? By living according to your word" (Psalm 119:9). Even as Jesus resisted and overcame temptation by reciting Scripture (Matthew 4:1-11), we need to immerse ourselves in the Word and learn to depend on its transforming power.

There are two main ways to do this:

1. *Spend some time reading the Bible on a daily basis.* This might sound cliché, but don't under-estimate the extent to which this simple practice can have a profound effect on your life.

2. *Memorize and meditate on Bible verses.* Choose verses you can employ against the specific lies and thought patterns you come up against.

Memorizing Scripture does not only affect us spiritually. It affects the biology of our brains as well. Memorization literally rewires our brains to think more like the way God thinks and love more like the way God loves. Living in a pornographic culture, our brains have been conformed to the pattern of this world. We are hardwired to view men as objectifiers, women as objects, and sexual intimacy as a product to be consumed. We have been told twisted stories about what our sexuality is and is for. Furthermore, our natural default setting is to gratify our sexual desires selfishly. We need to be transformed by the renewing of our minds (Romans 12:2). This happens as the living and active Word of God saturates our brains and infuses our thought lives with truth.

Sexual brokenness is not as much a condition of the body as it is a condition of the brain. As Neil T. Anderson explains, we need to obey the biblical command to "be transformed by the renewing of your mind" (Romans 12:2) until our brains learn to reject the enemy's lies and embrace God's truth.

Can strongholds of sexual bondage in the mind be broken? Yes! If our minds have been programmed wrongly, they can be reprogrammed....

In most cases, the root problem has proven to be a spiritual battle for their minds.

If Satan can get us to believe a lie, he will gain some measure of control over our feelings and behavior. He is intent on destroying a proper perception of God, of ourselves, of members of the opposite sex—including our spouses—and the world we live in. Our problems don't just stem from what we have believed in the past. Paul says we are to presently and continuously take every thought captive and make it obedient to Christ (see 2 Corinthians 10:5)....

Merely trying to stop thinking bad thoughts won't work. We must fill our minds with the pure, clear Word of God. There is no alternative plan. We overcome the father of lies by choosing the truth!

Neil T. Anderson, *Winning the Battle Within*

GETTING STARTED ON MEMORIZATION

Note: Your goal should be to memorize one verse each week.

1. Choose a verse (see table 4.1).

2. Read the verse aloud together.

3. Set aside a few minutes to memorize it.

4. Before you leave, read it aloud once more.

5. Write the verse on a note card or sticky note and place it where you will notice it several times a day (by your door, on a mirror, next to the desk).

6. If you're feeling creative, you can sing it, rap it, or paint it.

7. At the next weekly meeting, recite your verse by heart!

Table 4.1. Scripture verses for memorization

Psalm 4:8; 63:6—bedtime prayers	**2 Corinthians 10:3-5**—take every thought captive
Psalm 27—the Lord is my salvation	**Ephesians 4:22-24**—the old self versus the new self
Psalm 51—the prayer of a sexual sinner	**Ephesians 6:10-18**—put on the armor of God
Proverbs 7—warning against adultery	**Colossians 3:1-5**—set your hearts on things above
Matthew 4:1-11—the temptation of Jesus	**1 Thessalonians 4:3-8**—God's will for sexuality
Romans 8—no condemnation, no separation	**Hebrews 2:18; 4:15**—Savior for the tempted
1 Corinthians 6:18-20—flee sexual immorality	**1 John 1:5-10**—confess and walk in the light
1 Corinthians 10:13—God will provide a way out	**Revelation 12:11**—triumph over the serpent

REFLECTION

This week, try keeping track of your thought life every hour for one day. What thoughts tend to fill your mind, and how do they affect you sexually?

What lies do you find yourself believing?

What truths do you find to be powerful?

5

CONFESSION

*In confession we break through to the genuine community of the cross of
Jesus Christ.... It is grace that we can confess our sins to one another.*

DIETRICH BONHOEFFER, *LIFE TOGETHER*

In this group, you experienced the power of confession on a large scale when you shared
your sexual history and faced the wounds of your past. Now it's time to put confession into
practice in daily life. Confession is one of the most important skills you'll need to break free from
sexual sin and shame.

Spoiler alert: you don't have to wait until after sexually sinning to confess. The beautiful part
is that we can confess struggles and temptations *before* we actually sin! Too often, confession
becomes something we do *after* sexually acting out. But we don't need to wait. By confessing
more than just our sins, and by confessing before we sin, we can actually avoid sin. In confession,
earlier is always better.

REVIEW. In the case study we looked at
last time, at what point do you think the
person would have felt the need to confess
something, compared to when they actually
crossed into sin?

REFRAME. Confession takes practice. It
requires us to make a habit of exposing areas
of darkness in our hearts to one another, so
that we can "walk in the light," as 1 John 1 commands. But for those who already do this, it's
easy to become more aware of our ongoing sin

than God's ongoing grace. Talking about sin all
the time can make us feel defeated or deflated
by the frequency of our wandering. This is why
confession must go together with affirmation:
authentic, specific, positive verbal affirmation
and encouragement. We do not only need to
confess the ways we see sin in ourselves; we
need to affirm the ways we see God at work in
one another! The twin disciplines of confession
and affirmation must go together. Without frequent confession, we fall into denial; without

Dietrich Bonhoeffer sees confession not as a spiritual chore but as an opportunity for Christians to experience the power of the gospel in community. He explains why confession needs to happen between people, not just between individuals and God:

> Why is it that it is often easier for us to confess our sins to God than to a brother? God is holy and sinless, He is a just judge of evil and the enemy of all disobedience. But a brother is sinful as we are. He knows from his own experience the dark night of secret sin. Why should we not find it easier to go to a brother than to the holy God? But if we do, we must ask ourselves whether we have not often been deceiving ourselves with our confession of sin to God, whether we have not rather been confessing our sins to ourselves and also granting ourselves absolution. . . . Who can give us the certainty that, in the confession and the forgiveness of our sins, we are not dealing with ourselves but with the living God? God gives us this certainty through our brother. Our brother breaks the circle of self-deception. A man who confesses his sins in the presence of a brother knows that he is no longer alone with himself; he experiences the presence of God in the reality of the other person.
>
> Dietrich Bonhoeffer, *Life Together*

frequent affirmation, we fall into discouragement. But by talking transparently both about our own weaknesses and one another's strengths, we create a healthy environment for genuine spiritual growth.

Take this session as an opportunity to confess what we have done, and to affirm what God has done. When we do these things, we walk in the light.

READ. 1 John 1:5-10.

God is light; in him there is no darkness at all. If we claim to have fellowship with him and yet walk in the darkness, we lie and do not live out the truth. But if we walk in the light, as he is in the light, we have fellowship with one another, and the blood of Jesus, his Son, purifies us from all sin.

If we claim to be without sin, we deceive ourselves and the truth is not in us. If we confess our sins, he is faithful and just and will forgive us our sins and purify us from all unrighteousness. If we claim we have not sinned, we make him out to be a liar and his word is not in us.

REQUEST. Holy Spirit, help us to be real with one another on a daily basis. Keep reminding us of what Jesus has done, and how his light shines in our darkness, and the darkness has not overcome it. Amen.

EFFECTIVE CONFESSION

When done properly, confession leads to deeper self-awareness and genuine repentance. But not all confessions succeed at doing this. Learning what makes a confession effective or ineffective can help you gain traction on the road to sexual recovery. There is a big difference between confessing and confessing *well*.

The first step is to realize what confession is and is not. To confess simply means to tell the truth about something, even if that something is ugly, scary, or difficult to admit. Confession is not *limited* to sin. We can confess our

- desires
- struggles
- weaknesses
- temptations
- experiences
- memories
- emotions
- thoughts
- actions
- beliefs

These things are not sinful in themselves. What matters, then, is what we do with them. We can either try to face difficult events and emotions alone, or we can tell the truth about what's going on to a trusted friend. It does not only matter *that* we do this but *how* we do this. In table 5.1 you'll find a list of differences between effective and ineffective confessions. Which of the items accurately describe tendencies you see in your own life, good or bad?

Table 5.1. Effective versus ineffective confession

EFFECTIVE CONFESSION	INEFFECTIVE CONFESSION
• is completely honest, no pretending	• tries to make things look better
• is spoken out loud to a safe person	• is not spoken out loud to anyone
• tells the full background story in detail	• focuses only on the moment itself
• reveals thoughts, desires, and emotions	• focuses only on sinful behaviors
• takes enough time to process and pray	• is hurried up or rushed through
• reaches out during the time of need	• waits a few days to reach out
• turns away from sin (repentance)	• does not seek to change

LEVELS OF CONFESSION

Recall your most recent confession. What level would it fall into? Mark the spot on figure 5.1. Which is the next level of confession you want to hit?

NEXT STEP: PRACTICING AFFIRMATION

When we verbally acknowledge how we see evidence of God in each other, we give and receive a powerful energy boost on the road to sexual freedom and healing. The Bible says it best: "The tongue has the power of life and death" (Proverbs 18:21). Our words are powerful: "Therefore encourage one another and build each other up, just as in fact you are doing" (1 Thessalonians 5:11). It's a good rule to practice affirmation just as much as confession. So let's use our words to speak life, to build each other up, and to tear down the lies of the accuser.

Practice your affirmation skills using the following exercise.

1. Find a ball of yarn or a long rope.

2. Pass affirmations (with the yarn or rope) back and forth around the circle. Each person continues to hold onto the yarn or rope as it is passed to another person. Make sure everyone around the circle receives plenty of affirmation. After a few passes, this will create a visible web of affirmation.

3. Ask yourself this question until your turn comes around: *Who might I want to affirm? How have I seen Christ in this person?*

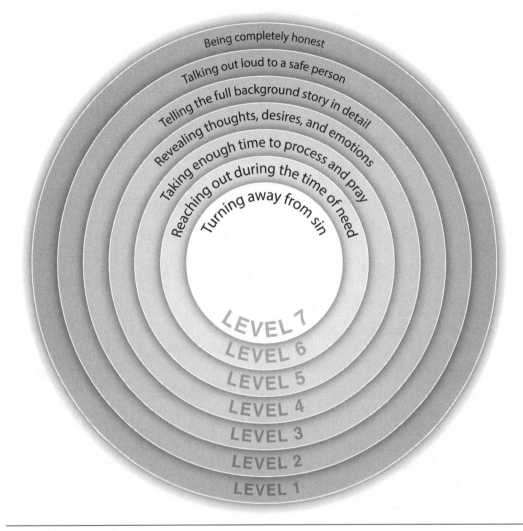

Figure 5.1. Levels of confession

REFLECTION

What tends to keep you from reaching out to others when you need them most?

How has it been to talk more honestly and openly about your sexuality in this group?

THEME TWO

IDENTITY

(6)

THE WOUNDED SELF

✳ ━━━━━━━━━━━━━━━━━━━━━━━━━━━━━━━━━━━━ ◄◄◄◄

To condemn someone who is in the midst of a shame cycle only makes
matters worse. If they are unable to hear that they have value as
a child of God, they cannot progress toward recovery.

WILLIAM STRUTHERS, *WIRED FOR INTIMACY*

Under the surface of sexual brokenness and temptation is the deeper issue of self-image and identity.

Experts acknowledge that unless a person's fundamental self-perception begins to change, destructive sexual patterns will remain in place. This session will reveal how we get stuck in destructive cycles of sexual brokenness, and how we can break free into a cycle of healing and redemption by receiving the truth of what God says about us.

REVIEW. As you practiced confession this week, what patterns did you notice in your sexual thoughts and behaviors?

REFRAME. Sexual behavior, whether healthy or unhealthy, begins in the brain and follows predictable patterns. These patterns become cycles that repeat themselves until they are totally streamlined. In other words, you can get to a point where your sexual behavior (good or bad) becomes automatic; you don't even have to think about it anymore. The bad news is that this makes it incredibly difficult to break free from sexual bondage. The good news is that once you initiate a healthy cycle of sexual behavior, it gets

easier and easier to continue over time. Once you are familiar with how cycles of sexual behavior work, you'll begin to notice them in your own life. You'll notice when something or someone triggers your *wounded self* toward sin, and how God can bring you back to your senses through the truth of your *redeemed self*.

READ. Ephesians 4:22-24.

You were taught, with regard to your former way of life, to put off your old self, which is being corrupted by its deceitful desires; to be made new in the attitude of your minds; and to put on the new self, created to be like God in true righteousness and holiness.

REQUEST. Jesus, you have buried our old selves and made us new creations. Strengthen us through your Spirit to break free from any chains weighing us down. Purify our thoughts and actions as we pursue righteousness and holiness together as sexual people who are created in your image. Amen.

CYCLES OF SEXUAL BEHAVIOR

Using the language of "cycles of sexual behavior" is a way to describe complex neurobiological processes at work. It communicates basic concepts about how our brains work to those of us who are not neuroscientists. In *Wired for Intimacy*, William Struthers explains cyclical sexual behavior with the metaphor of traveling down a road.

Imagine that you could be neurologically "enslaved" to purity rather than porn. Enslaved to seeing the dignity of each individual rather than their utility to you. This is the distinction between the journey toward sanctification and the journey toward depravity. As you travel farther along either road, you pick up momentum and it becomes harder to turn around. The farther down the road you travel, the less opportunity you have to deviate from the road as it narrows. The road of depravity leads into the heart of hell and yields isolation. The road to sanctification, however, leads into the heart of God and yields freedom from temptation.

Sexual cycles operate on this principle known as neuroplasticity. It means that the further you go in each cycle (whether sexual addiction or sexual redemption), the easier it is to continue as time goes on. At first, it will be really hard to break the old cycle. The old cycle is familiar. The brain is used to traveling that path repeatedly. It will take time to forge a new path and get used to the new cycle, but eventually it becomes second nature. Because our brains are able to change, there is incredible hope for real transformation!

As a group, read through the two sets of sexual core beliefs (fig. 6.1).

CORE BELIEFS OF THE SEXUALLY ADDICTED	CORE BELIEFS OF THE SEXUALLY REDEEMED
1. I am a bad, unworthy person.	1. I am a son or daughter of the Most High King.
2. No one can love me as I am.	2. I am unconditionally loved by God and others.
3. No one can take care of my needs but me.	3. My needs can be met in healthy, positive ways.
4. Sex is my most important need.	4. I do not need sex to enjoy life and intimacy.

Figure 6.1. Sexual core beliefs

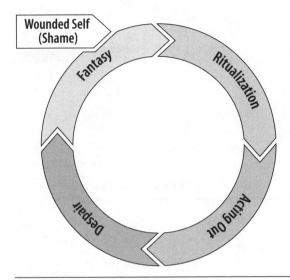

CYCLE OF SEXUAL ADDICTION

Wounded Self: Old, negative self-image based on lies (e.g., *I am a worthless piece of trash.*)

Fantasy: Preoccupation with a false vision of beauty (e.g., the inviting smile of a porn star)

Ritualization: The steps I take so that I can act out (e.g., I go to my room, I turn on the computer)

Acting out: Lustful, sexually destructive behaviors (e.g., watching porn, masturbating, intercourse)

Despair: Feeling defeated, leading back into shame (e.g., *I already failed, so why not do it again?*)

Figure 6.2. Cycle of sexual addiction

Lies of My Wounded Self

Examine the cycle of sexual addiction. Then in groups of two or three, outline what this cycle looks like in your own life using the space below.

Sexual fantasy leading me to lust:

Ritualization (bad rituals):

Sinful behaviors (bad results):

Voice of shame and despair:

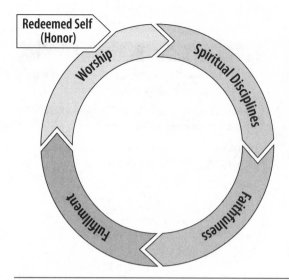

Figure 6.3. Cycle of sexual redemption

Truth of My Redeemed Self

Examine the cycle of sexual redemption (fig. 6.3). Then in groups of two or three, outline what the cycle looks like in your own life using the space below.

Reality of God leading me to worship:

Spiritual disciplines (good rituals):

Faithful behaviors (good results):

Voice of honor and fulfillment:

NEXT STEP:
HEALTHY BODY IMAGE

An important part of learning to "put on the new self" as God's beloved children is learning to affirm our physical bodies as good and valuable. To reject or devalue our bodies is to reject and devalue the very work of God, who creates and sustains them. When we look at our bodies with contempt, we are acting as though God made a mistake. We need to see ourselves, including our bodies, the way he sees us: through the lens of love.

To begin, draw a picture of your body. On your drawing, indicate

- a part of your body you particularly enjoy
- a part of your body you wish was different

On a separate sheet of paper, write a letter to God about your body. Tell him how you really feel about it. Express doubts, give thanks, ask hard questions, appreciate wonderful parts, lament broken parts.

Don't forget to talk about the sexual parts. He cares about your whole body, including those parts. Then imagine how God might reply to your letter, and write a letter back to yourself from him!

REFLECTION

What helps you to "put off the old self" and "put on the new self"?

How might God see your body differently than you see your body?

(7)

IDENTITY IN CHRIST

*The major strategy of Satan is to distort the character of God
and the truth of who we are. He can't change God and he can't do anything
to change our identity and position in Christ. If, however, he can get us to
believe a lie, we will live as though our identity in Christ isn't true.*

NEIL T. ANDERSON, *VICTORY OVER THE DARKNESS*

In this session we will talk about the most important piece of this curriculum: how God relates to us as sexually broken and sinful people. He not only forgives us; he lovingly embraces and delights in us as his own sons and daughters. His love tells us who we are, heals our hearts, renews our minds, changes our behavior, and transforms our brokenness into sexual wholeness.

REVIEW. When you are in the middle of sexual sin or shame, what expression do you imagine is on God's face as he looks at you? (Angry? Disappointed? Distant? Neutral? Tolerant? Pleased?)

REFRAME. How we imagine God relates to us determines how we relate to him. Unfortunately, many of us have bought into the idea that God reacts negatively to sexually sinful and broken people. Jesus Christ met many such people in his life and ministry; never once did he shy away or condemn. He loved and accepted them as they were, yet he did not leave them as they were. All who touched him were transformed. Jesus demonstrates how

God's fundamental posture to human beings, no matter how sexually sinful or broken, is one of relentless, overpowering love.

READ. John 15:9; 1 John 3:1.

As the Father has loved me, so have I loved you. Now remain in my love.

See what great love the Father has lavished on us, that we should be called children of God! And that is what we are!

REQUEST. Father, thank you for embracing us with such great love. Take the truth of our adoption as your children and make it real to our hearts. Open up our eyes to see the beauty of your Son, and the truth of who we are in him. Amen.

THE DOUBLE LIE

In order to be clear about how God relates to us in our sexual struggles, we first need to be clear about how God does *not* relate to us. God never tempts us (James 1:13) or heaps condemnation on us (Romans 8:1). Even so, it can be easy to confuse the voice of God with a voice that keeps us trapped in sexual shame and sin. We can distinguish between the two by recognizing one of the enemy's most effective strategies: the double lie.

The double lie begins with *temptation*, minimizing the seriousness of sin and the holiness of God: *Who cares? God will still forgive you. You want this so badly. Just give in. You'll be fine.*

Sounds familiar. But then, once you listen to that voice and give in to temptation, it will turn on you. That same voice switches to *accusation*, minimizing the grace of the gospel and the love of God: *You failed again! Are you even a Christian? Who do you think you are? You're pathetic!*

This voice does not come from God. How do we know this for sure? Because it contradicts itself. Its two messages are completely incompatible, and yet somehow we tend to believe both of them. By listening to the double lie, we are defeated by the enemy not *once* but *twice*. Exposing the double lie reveals who this voice *really* comes from: Satan, who "when he lies, he speaks his native language, for he is a liar and the father of lies" (John 8:44). Sometimes we

wobble back and forth from one side of the double lie to the other: from *temptation* to *accusation* and back again. We get stuck.

How have you personally experienced the double lie?

THE DOUBLE TRUTH

The gospel of Jesus Christ defeats the double lie, both in temptation and in accusation (see fig. 7.1). When we are sexually tempted, the gospel gives us God's power; when we are sexually ashamed, the gospel gives us God's pardon. It tells us the double truth that though we may be great sinners, Christ is a greater Savior. While the double lie focuses our attention on what we are doing, the gospel focuses our attention on who Jesus is and who we are because of what he did for us.

Against temptation, the gospel says, "You're right: even if you sin, God won't turn away from you. But he suffered and died specifically to set you free from this. Look at Christ: crucified for you, buried for you, risen for you! Will you now walk in your identity as one who belongs to him?"

Against accusation, the gospel says, "You're right: you're not worthy of the Father's love and you never have been. But he loves you still. You are his delight. God is your Father, Jesus is your brother, and the Holy Spirit lives in you. Will you accept your status as his beloved child?"

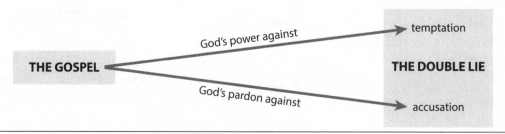

Figure 7.1. The gospel versus the double lie

WHO AM I IN CHRIST?

The gospel defeats the double lie by giving us a new identity in Christ. After all, if Jesus is who he says he is, then we are who he says we are. The list of statements on the following pages highlights this truth. People often find this list especially helpful for responding to the double lie. Quietly read through the list and mark the identity statements that are most meaningful for you.

Who Am I in Christ?

I am loved.	(John 15:9)	I am a sister of Christ.	(Hebrews 2:11)
I am clean.	(John 15:3)	I am alive with Christ.	(Ephesians 2:5)
I am free.	(John 8:36)	I am a new creation.	(2 Corinthians 5:17)
I am secure.	(John 10:29)	I am dead to sin.	(Romans 6:11)
I am a saint.	(Ephesians 1:1)	I am no longer condemned.	(Romans 8:1)
I am forgiven.	(Ephesians 1:7)	I am more than a conqueror.	(Romans 8:37)
I am included.	(Ephesians 2:19)	I am a slave of righteousness.	(Romans 6:19)
I am complete.	(Ephesians 3:19)	I am chosen and dearly loved.	(Colossians 3:12)
I am delivered.	(Colossians 1:13)	I am a member of Christ's body.	(1 Corinthians 12:27)
I am redeemed.	(Galatians 3:13)	I am the righteousness of God.	(2 Corinthians 5:21)
I am blameless.	(Colossians 1:22)	I am a minister of reconciliation.	(2 Corinthians 5:18)
I am not alone.	(Matthew 28:20)	I am an ambassador of Christ.	(2 Corinthians 5:20)
I am a child of God.	(John 1:12)	I am a branch of the true vine.	(John 15:1)
I am Christ's friend.	(John 15:15)	I am a sheep of the good Shepherd.	(John 10:16)
I am a holy temple.	(1 Corinthians 6:19)	I am united with other believers.	(John 17:23)
I am an heir of God.	(Galatians 4:6-7)	I am prayed for by Christ himself.	(Hebrews 7:25)
I am a citizen of heaven.	(Philippians 3:20)	I am healed by his wounds.	(1 Peter 2:24)
I am a brother of Christ.	(Hebrews 2:11)	I am God's masterpiece.	(Ephesians 2:10)

What Happened to Me?

I have been justified.	(Romans 5:1)	I have been chosen before the creation of the world.	(Ephesians 1:4)
I have been adopted.	(Ephesians 1:5)	I have been delivered from the domain of darkness.	(Colossians 1:13)
I have been qualified.	(Colossians 1:12)	I have been brought into the kingdom of the Son.	(Colossians 1:13)
I have been forgiven.	(Colossians 1:14)	I have been brought near to God through Christ's blood.	(Ephesians 2:13)
I have been reconciled.	(2 Corinthians 5:18)	I have been shown the incomparable riches of God's grace.	(Ephesians 2:7)
I have been crucified with Christ.	(Galatians 2:20)	I have been given God's grace lavishly and without restriction.	(Ephesians 1:8)
I have been buried with Christ.	(Colossians 2:12)	I have been born of God, and the evil one cannot touch me.	(1 John 5:18)
I have been raised with Christ.	(Colossians 2:12)	I have not received a spirit of fear, but of power, love, and self-discipline.	(2 Timothy 1:7)
I have been made alive with Christ.	(Colossians 2:13)		
I have been firmly rooted in Christ.	(Colossians 2:7)		
I have been completed by Christ.	(Colossians 2:10)		
I have been anointed by God.	(2 Corinthians 1:21)		
I have been given the Holy Spirit.	(2 Corinthians 1:22)		
I have been redeemed from the curse of the law.	(Galatians 3:13)		
I have been blessed with every spiritual blessing.	(Ephesians 1:3)		

What Happened to Me? (continued)

I have been created in Christ to do the work he has prepared for me to do.	(Ephesians 2:10)	I have been bought with a price. I am not my own. I belong to God.	(1 Corinthians 6:20)

What Do I Have?

I have hope.	(Colossians 1:27)	I have the Holy Spirit.	(1 Corinthians 2:12)
I have peace.	(Ephesians 2:14)	I have a great high priest.	(Hebrews 4:14)
I have purpose.	(Romans 8:28)	I have the mind of Christ.	(1 Corinthians 2:16)
I have victory.	(1 Corinthians 15:57)	I have access to the Father.	(Ephesians 2:18)
I have eternal life.	(John 6:47)	I have the full armor of God.	(Ephesians 6:11)

And When Christ Returns

I will be just like him!	(1 John 3:2)

- Allow time for each member of the group to share two or three of their favorite statements.

- Optional: Choose one or two statements to meditate on and memorize during the week—write these down on a separate piece of paper and display them someplace where you will be regularly reminded of these truths.

It is essential for us to accept and appropriate our identity as God's beloved sons and daughters in order to disrupt cycles of sexual shame and sin. We need to see ourselves first and foremost as people loved by God in Jesus Christ, a love that Michael Lawrence describes this way:

> We can say "God loves you" all day long and it won't make a dent, because people know deep down that God's love is not deserved. But when I'm told that God loves Christ, and that I've been adopted in Christ by faith, I now have something to put my confidence in, something that isn't contradicted by my knowledge of myself. Christian, you are loved, not because you're lovely or obedient, but because Christ is lovely and obedient, and you are in Christ. You have been adopted. . . . It shouldn't surprise us that in the biblical language of sons and daughters, we find a powerful antidote to a deadly poison. But in fact, in our identity as sons and daughters of God we've been given something far more powerful than an antidote to the failings of our time. We've been given an identity that calls us beyond ourselves and our emotional needs to the story of the glory of God.

Michael Lawrence, "Biblical Theology and Identity"

WHO ARE *WE* IN CHRIST?

It is not only important to realize our identity in Christ as individuals but to realize our corporate identity as God's people, the church. The gospel not only transforms the way we see ourselves, it transforms the way we see and relate to each other as brothers, sisters, and image-bearers.

1. *We are all created in the image of God* (Genesis 1:27). We matter, and what we do matters. By creating us in his image, God has given us inestimable value, worth, and significance. Even the people we are tempted to objectify have been created in God's image, and how we treat them is how we treat God. We are his artwork.

2. *We are all equally fallen and broken* (Romans 3:23). We are always in need of grace, no matter what. We never reach a point where we no longer need the gospel or the grace of God. Therefore, we should not be surprised when we find ourselves to be more sinful and selfish than we previously thought. We are rebels.

3. *We are all equally loved by the Father* (1 John 3:1). We are loved by God so much that we can do absolutely nothing to increase or decrease his love for us. The truest thing about us is that we are his beloved children, in whom he is well-pleased. Nothing and no one is beyond his embrace. We are his delight.

4. *We are all equally redeemed by Christ* (Ephesians 1:7). We are now in Christ, who purchased us, purified us, and put his Spirit in us. In him our old selves have been crucified on the cross, and in him our new selves have now been raised from the dead. He shed his blood to make us holy. We belong to him now.

5. *We are all equally recipients of the Spirit* (Ephesians 4:4). We are all ministers of the Holy Spirit. God chooses to dwell in us, lead us into all truth, and use us in each other's lives for his glory. With God as our Father, Jesus as our brother, and the Holy Spirit living in us, we have everything we need. We are equipped.

6. *We are all members of the body of Christ* (1 Corinthians 12:27). We are dependent on one another in order to truly reflect Christ. We cannot spiritually thrive apart from community. God designed the body so that every part is necessary for the health and growth of the whole. We cannot work alone; we need each other.

7. *We are all destined for eternity with God* (Revelation 21:3). We are all headed for the greatest wedding that there will ever be: the marriage supper of the Lamb.

When Christ comes back to take us home, we will be completely transformed. On that day, we will have new bodies and there will be no sin. We have hope.

We are God's flock.	(1 Peter 5:2)
We are God's family.	(Romans 8:17)
We are children of light.	(Ephesians 5:8)
We are the bride of Christ.	(John 3:29)
We are a royal priesthood.	(1 Peter 2:9)
We are a holy nation.	(1 Peter 2:9)
We are the church.	(Acts 20:28)

NEXT STEP: THE VOICE OF JESUS

On the road to sexual freedom and healing in Christ, sometimes we grow discouraged. We lose sight of Jesus and the never-ending grace he lavishes on us. Especially after periods of great progress, the moments when we turn back to the old ways of the wounded self can be devastating. By now you have probably had a few slips (one-time setbacks) or relapses (strings of multiple setbacks) in which you acted out sexually. You probably felt horrible and gross. These experiences of defeat can make us feel disqualified from God's love and renew the shame cycle. In the midst of sexual relapses, how does God relate to us? What does the voice of Jesus say?

Choose to engage with one of the following Scripture passages as a way of connecting the voice of Jesus to sexual sin. Enter deeply into the passage you choose; don't rush or try to read them all.

John 8:1-11

1. Read the passage out loud together.

2. Imagine yourself in the place of the woman caught in adultery (or that you are there with her, watching it happen). What do you see? What is going through your mind? How do you feel?

3. Read the passage out loud together again from this perspective.

4. Imagine yourself in the place of Jesus this time (or that you are a face in the crowd, watching Jesus). What do you see? What is going through your mind? How do you feel?

5. Read the passage out loud together one last time, slowly and carefully.

6. Respond in prayer to the voice of Jesus: "Neither do I condemn you. Go now and leave your life of sin."

Luke 7:36-50

1. Read the passage out loud together.

2. Imagine you are the sinful woman. Around the room, hard eyes are judging you. How do you feel?

3. Imagine you are the Pharisee. Why do you look down on this woman? What makes you superior?

4. Imagine you are Jesus. You see her sins, and you see her love for you. How do you feel about her?

5. Imagine you are the woman again. You hear Jesus' parable about the moneylender and the debtors. In front of everyone, he rebukes the Pharisee and honors you, to your surprise. Can you believe it?

6. Jesus looks the Pharisee in the eye and says, "Her many sins have been forgiven." Then he says to you, softly: "Your sins are forgiven. Your faith has saved you; go in peace." How do you react?

7. Respond in prayer to the voice of Jesus: "Whoever has been forgiven little loves little."

Romans 5–8

1. Divide the four chapters of Romans 5–8 among groups of one or two people.

2. In groups, read your chapter, underline key verses, and summarize ideas.

3. Listen to each group present their summaries of Romans 5, 6, 7, or 8.

4. Respond in prayer to any verses that stood out to you in Romans 5–8.

The voice of Jesus corrects, but never condemns. The voice of Jesus commands, but never coerces. The voice of Jesus is tender and true, holy and healing, gracious and good. It is the voice of love. The voice of Jesus brings freedom, not fear; peace, not pride; shalom, not shame. It brings life.

REFLECTION

What does the double lie say to you when you are tempted or ashamed?

Which identity statement speaks most powerfully to you right now?

8

FACING TEMPTATION

*The line between temptation and sin can seem blurry. But when
we view both from a biblical lens, we see that temptation is not sin,
unless acted upon with sinful thoughts, behaviors, and desires.*

ELLEN DYKAS, *SEXUAL SANITY FOR WOMEN*

A temptation is not a trespass; it is a test. In sexual temptation, we're given a test of whether or not we will choose to live as sons and daughters of God—our true identity. It's a choice between embracing the new, redeemed self or giving in to the old, wounded self. We can either give in to the old self by returning to old sexual patterns or live in the reality of the new self by embracing patterns of sexual holiness and health instead. Yet it's never as easy as it sounds. Temptation has a way of convincing us to live in fearful silence instead of vulnerability, to live in shame instead of in our identity in Christ, and to live in isolation instead of intimacy with those who would love to connect with us if only we reached out for help. Temptation is a test we cannot hope to pass on our own. But together with God and one other, we can learn to face it and even to overcome it.

REVIEW. What is one situation that often leads you into sexual temptation?

REFRAME. In the temptation of Jesus (Matthew 4:1-11; Luke 4:1-13), we see how temptation is a challenge to his identity. Satan begins the first two temptations by saying, "If you are the Son of God . . ." He tries to cast a shadow over what the Father had just said: "This is my Son, whom I love; with him I am well pleased" (Matthew 3:17). He offers Jesus

comfort, control, and significance apart from his identity and mission as God's beloved. In response to each temptation, Jesus responds by quoting Scripture, saying "It is written . . ." Not even Jesus fights temptation with his own willpower. Instead, he relies on the Father's voice, the Spirit's leading, and the truth of God's Word. So when it comes to facing sexual temptation, Jesus is our model and master teacher. As Hebrews 2:18 tells us, "Because he himself suffered when he was tempted, he is able to help those who are being tempted." Through his power, we have a way out of even the toughest temptations!

READ. 1 Corinthians 10:13.

> No temptation has overtaken you except what is common to mankind. And God is faithful; he will not let you be tempted beyond what you can bear. But when you are tempted, he will also provide a way out so that you can endure it.

REQUEST. Holy Spirit, don't let us think so much of ourselves that we try to defeat temptation on our own. Also don't let us think so little of ourselves that we give up and give in. Teach us to stay close to you and let you do the fighting for us. Lead us not into temptation, but deliver us from evil. Amen.

TEMPTATION DIALOGUE

Sometimes we feel embarrassed just to admit when we are feeling tempted. In reality, being able to talk about our temptations (especially while going through them) is a mark of spiritual and emotional maturity. Those of us who have especially strong, strange, or disturbing experiences of temptation find ourselves in good company: Jesus "has been tempted in every way, just as we are—yet he did not sin" (Hebrews 4:15). Surely "in every way" includes all kinds of sexually tempting thoughts and desires. No matter the nature of your sexual struggle, Jesus can empathize with you as one who experienced it fully and yet never sinned.

In order to better understand and respond to sexual temptation, each of us will write out our own personal temptation dialogue. This is an emotionally intense activity. It requires you to get into the enemy's head and come face-to-face with the darkness within. You can expect to be surprised and even unsettled by realizing the thoughts that actually go through your mind when you are sexually tempted. You might not want to write them down. Don't let this stop you from engaging. Let this exercise increase your self-awareness so that when the real thing comes, you'll be prepared.

1. Write your name in the blank "The Temptation of _____."

2. Imagine a setting that would be especially sexually tempting for you.

Time and place. In what real-life situation would you be faced with intense sexual temptation?

Triggers. What triggers might set you off? Triggers can be physical (I was lying in bed and couldn't fall asleep), mental (I thought back to my old relationship), or emotional (I felt lonely, depressed, and exhausted). *Note:* Triggers cannot force you to sin. They can only present you with thoughts, images, or ideas. Ultimately, you have a choice of whether or not to pull the trigger.

3. Write a realistic dialogue between your own voice and the voice of temptation. Don't write what you *should* say in response; write what you typically *tend* to say.

You can include elements such as (1) false messages like the narrative of your wounded self, and both sides of the double lie, and (2) stages of the sexual cycle (shame, preoccupation, ritualization, acting out, despair).

Remember: because sin is so much more than outward behavior, your temptation may or may not include sexually acting out. It could simply mean dwelling on inappropriate thoughts, allowing feelings to take control, listening to lies instead of truth, or sexually acting in (repressing our sexuality out of fear)—anything to prevent us from whatever God is calling us to do at the time.

The Temptation of _____

The Setting:

Time and place:

Triggers (physical, mental, or emotional):

Voice of Temptation	*My Response*

One of the best strategies against temptation is identifying and avoiding the triggers that feed into it. We can begin to do this by looking at our own triggers and understanding how they work. Marnie Ferree explains the concept of triggers and how they function as gateways to sexual temptation:

> A trigger may be a reminder of something in the past, either something that's positive or negative. Some triggers remind us of pain of some sort whether physical, emotional or spiritual. For example, we see a TV show or movie about abuse that's similar to what we experienced, and we're vividly put in touch with that vulnerable little girl who was hurt. Or a friend ignores us for some reason, and we're emotionally kicked back into that wounded place of growing up in a family where we didn't feel like we mattered. . . . Whatever the particular pain, a trigger inflames and intensifies it in the present moment. . . .
>
> Stress can also play a huge part in the process. When we feel anxious, lonely, pressured or exhausted because of stress of any kind, we want to soothe that uncomfortable state. We're tense and wound up and want to calm down. Many of us have discovered that nicotine or alcohol will calm our mood with their depressant effect. We've also discovered sexual activity will do the same thing—and usually better.
>
> Marnie C. Ferree, *No Stones*

NEXT STEP: LEGALISM AND LICENSE

When trying to overcome sexual temptation, we often flip-flop between two extremes: legalism (self-righteousness) and license (self-indulgence).

See figure 8.1 to take a closer look at these two extremes.

LEGALISM	LICENSE
Motivation = guilt and self-righteousness	*Motivation* = greed and self-indulgence
Source of power: the voice of accusation	*Source of power:* the voice of temptation
Looks like: sexual repression	*Looks like:* sexual hedonism
• "I better stay pure this time, or else . . ."	• "It's not a big deal, God doesn't mind."
• "God will be disappointed with me if I sin again."	• "Ultimately it's okay if I sin; God will forgive me."
• "If I do give in, I should be ashamed of myself."	• "If I do give in, it's better to take it less seriously."
Leads to: perfectionism, counting the days since acting out, frustration, exhaustion, burning out, less perceived need for grace, less appreciation for the magnitude of God's unconditional love	*Leads to:* apathy, stagnation, lowering standards, spiritual numbness, loss of motivation, less appetite for truth, less appreciation for the magnitude of God's enormous holiness
Also known as: sin management	*Also known as:* cheap grace

Figure 8.1. Extremes of legalism and license

Sexual recovery groups often start out with a legalistic attitude of sin management, of trying to stop sexually sinning—which inevitably becomes stressful and ultimately unhelpful. When groups realize that legalism doesn't actually work, they swivel in the opposite direction to a licentious attitude of cheap grace, of easy forgiveness and lower standards, which inevitably becomes stagnant. But the gospel denies both legalism and license, and gives us a third way to respond to sexual temptation based on the love of Christ (see fig. 8.2).

LOVE
Motivation = gratitude and self-giving
Source of power: the voice of Jesus
Looks like: sexual faithfulness
• "I am God's beloved child; I don't need sex to feel better about myself."
• "I live by faith in the Son of God, who loved me and gave himself for me."
• "Even when I'm unfaithful to God, he is still faithful and never gives up on me."
Leads to: worship, heart change, commitment to God and others, ongoing growth, becoming Christlike
Also known as: the gospel

Figure 8.2. The way of love

The gospel does not lower our standards (license) or demand that we meet God's standards (legalism). Instead, it tells us that God's standards are infinitely higher than we could ever hope to live up to, and Christ meets every single one of them for us, in our place. This fills our hearts and invites us to respond with our whole lives, including our sexuality. In the gospel, we are given the power to relate to others not in lust but with the love that we ourselves have received from God.

Discuss: Is this group more prone toward legalism or license? What about you personally? How does the gospel defeat both sexual legalism and sexual license?

LEGALISM, LICENSE, OR LOVE?

See if you can classify the following sentences as coming from a heart of legalism, license, or love (reference the previous page if you need to).

- I'm not content with my sexual thoughts and habits; they're really hindering my relationship with God.

- It's been two months since I looked at porn—I can't believe I've been clean for this long!

- I went home and messed up again. I always do this. Sometimes I wonder if I'm even growing at all.

- When I think about Jesus and what he did for me, I don't want to go back to my old ways anymore.

- I know I haven't been following my recovery plan, but I'm just too busy to spend time in God's Word.

- My mind has been full of lustful fantasies lately, but hey, at least I haven't masturbated.

- I want to be a great spouse and lover one day, someone who can be truly satisfied with my partner.

- I hate the way porn always makes me feel. I just want to be done with it and feel better.

- Every time one of us fails against temptation, we will all go on a fast together for twenty-four hours.

- I feel like watching pornography doesn't hurt anyone; it just helps release energy and get my mind off of things.

- I'm sick of always comparing how attractive people are. I want to see my brothers and sisters as God sees them.

- I know Jesus has grace for me, but that doesn't help me. I need to be motivated by consequences or else I won't change.

- I can't stop thinking about what porn does to women. This is not just an issue of purity, it's an issue of injustice.

- At least I'm doing better than some people in our group. Maybe by summer, I won't have to try so hard to be pure.

REFLECTION

How does the enemy tend to trick you into giving into sexual temptation?

How does the gospel affect the way you approach sexual recovery?

9

CREATING A BATTLE PLAN

✳━━━⋘

Resist the devil, and he will flee from you.
Come near to God and he will come near to you.

JAMES 4:7-8

By this point, you've seen how sexual brokenness looks and works in your own life; you've also seen the power of your identity in Christ to overcome lies and sexual temptations. Now it's time to get practical. What will you actually *do* to put these things into practice? In the midst of your sexual struggles, there is a spiritual battle going on; you cannot afford to disengage. You need to create a battle plan.

REVIEW. What is one strategy you have found effective for overcoming sexual shame and sin?

REFRAME. Our battles against sexual sin and shame involve an element of spiritual warfare. While some Christians blame the bulk of their sexual struggles on demonic influences, others never acknowledge evil spiritual forces at all. Yet the Bible speaks plainly about the role played by Satan and demons in opposing the purposes of Jesus. This curriculum seeks to take a more balanced approach, realizing that evil exists both inside of us (individual sin) and outside of us (principalities and powers). Not all experiences of sexual temptation involve a demon, but some do. Our job is not necessarily

to figure out whether we are dealing with our own sinful desires or more sinister influences (or both). Rather, our role is to draw near to Jesus. We can't defeat sin or Satan on our own, but we can put ourselves in a position to depend on God's presence and power when we need it most. In spiritual warfare, we are not nearly strong enough to overcome the enemy—only God is! The strategies of spiritual warfare we will look at are the means God himself uses to deliver us. Listen to how Paul instructs believers to engage in spiritual warfare:

READ. Ephesians 6:10-17.

Finally, be strong in the Lord and in his mighty power. Put on the full armor of God, so that you can take your stand against the devil's schemes. For our struggle is not against flesh and blood, but against the rulers, against the authorities, against the powers of this dark world and against the spiritual forces of evil in the heavenly realms. Therefore put on the full armor of God, so that when the day of evil comes, you may be able to stand your ground, and after you have done everything, to stand. Stand firm then, with the belt of truth buckled around your waist, with the breastplate of righteousness in place, and with your feet fitted with the readiness that comes from the gospel of peace. In addition to all this, take up the shield of faith, with which you can extinguish all the flaming arrows of the evil one. Take the helmet of salvation and the sword of the Spirit, which is the word of God.

REQUEST. God our refuge and strength, we acknowledge that we are weak. Yet you say, "My power is made perfect in your weakness." We cannot win this battle alone. Yet you are with us and your Holy Spirit lives in us. Teach us to rely on you and on one another rather than ourselves, so that when we see victory, you get all the glory. Amen.

STRATEGIES FOR SPIRITUAL WARFARE

In this exercise, you will create a battle plan for engaging in spiritual warfare when you are tempted.

Because you face individually customized temptations, you need an individually customized strategy for victory. This plan needs to be based on biblical principles driven by God's grace or else it will turn into mere sin management and behavior modification. The question is: what effectively connects you to the presence and power of God? What jump-starts your heart to worship him, to say yes to him and no to sin? The goal is not simply to play defense against destructive actions, but to play offense in the power of his love and the freedom of obedience.

Step 1: The opposition. What are we up against? In spiritual warfare, we face internal *and* external opposition. Internally, we must confront our sinful nature (Romans 7:25); externally, we must confront "the spiritual forces of evil" (Ephesians 6:12).

Use the questions in figure 9.1 to identify the opposition you will be up against.

INTERNAL ENEMIES

Sins: What selfish attitudes and behaviors have I been experiencing?

Idols: What people or things might be taking God's place in my heart?

EXTERNAL ENEMIES

Accusations: What lies from the enemy continue to have an influence on me?

Temptations: What situations and strategies does "the tempter" use against me?

Figure 9.1. Internal and external enemies

Step 2: The arsenal. *What equipment do we have at our disposal?* The Bible gives us many strategies for spiritual warfare. After all, we have the full armor of God! However, there is no specific formula for achieving victory. The armor of God fits us all differently. Throughout this exercise, ask yourself, *What will work best for me personally, for me specifically?*

We will look at three types of tactics: preventative, offensive, and defensive.

1. *Preventative tactics: The pregame.* "I have hidden your word in my heart that I might not sin against you" (Psalm 119:11).

Preventative tactics are basically the little steps we can take daily to avoid temptation altogether. These include actions that keep us far from danger, and actions that keep us close to the Lord.

They are also known as "disciplines of abstinence" and "disciplines of engagement" (see fig. 9.2).

2. *Offensive tactics: Stand and fight!* Offensive tactics are ways we can actively access God's deliverance in the thick of temptation. These are directions for what to do when we find ourselves tempted, alone, and trapped. They are most effective when we want to obey God but don't feel like we have the power to resist evil. These tactics put us in touch with

God's power to drive out all darkness. Through them, we come to know and believe that "we are more than conquerors through him who loved us" (Romans 8:37). See figure 9.3 for tried and true offensive spiritual weapons.

3. *Defensive tactics: Flee!* "Flee from sexual immorality" (1 Corinthians 6:18). Defensive tactics are last-resort options for when we want to give in to sexual temptation and no longer trust our own judgment. In such moments the wisest thing to do is to leave the situation. How do you know when you've reached this point? It's different for every person. Some use the acronym HALT (hungry, angry, lonely, tired) to discern if they are in danger of sexually acting out. They know which feelings to watch for. If you are tempted to sexually act out with another person, defensive tactics will be especially important for you. There comes a point when you need to stop praying for sexual purity and start practicing it by walking away from a high-risk environment! Plan your escape route now, and ask the Lord to give you strength and courage to take it when the time of testing comes. Examples include leaving the house, working out, calling a prayer partner.

What defensive tactic helps you flee sexual danger?

DISCIPLINES OF ABSTINENCE	DISCIPLINES OF ENGAGEMENT
(Actions that keep me far from danger.)	*(Actions that keep me close to the Lord.)*
For example:	For example:
• Internet filters and restrictions	• Morning or evening devotions
• Deactivating Facebook or Instagram	• Scripture meditation or memorization
• Monitoring my private thought life	• Spending time with close friends
• Getting enough sleep at night	• Practicing rhythms of Sabbath
• Setting boundaries in dating	• Serving the needs of others
• Avoiding certain triggers	• Attending my small group
•	•
•	•

Figure 9.2. Disciplines of abstinence and engagement (include your own)

Step 3: The battle plan. Now what will we actually do? The following space is yours to create your own battle plan, based on the opposition you are facing and the tactics of spiritual warfare that will help you find victory. Once you have finished, make a copy of this plan to share with your prayer partner(s) and your leader. You may also want to create a small summary of your battle plan to put on an index card or take a picture of it to have on your phone.

The following is an example of what you might write as you develop your plan:

My opposition: Nightmares (When I wake up from a horrible dream in the middle of the night).

My strategy: Recite Psalm 4:8 before falling asleep. If I have a nightmare, call my prayer partner.

My Opposition

My Strategy

One phrase to summarize my overall strategy:

Speak the word of God (especially out loud)
- "The word of God is alive and active. Sharper than any double-edged sword." (Hebrews 4:12)
- "Take . . . the sword of the Spirit, which is the word of God." (Ephesians 6:17)

Call on the name of the Lord
- "The name of the Lord is a fortified tower; / the righteous run to it and are safe." (Proverbs 18:10)
- "They surrounded me on every side / but in the name of the Lord I cut them down." (Psalm 118:11)

Seek out another believer
- "Though one may be overpowered, / two can defend themselves. / A cord of three strands is not quickly broken." (Ecclesiastes 4:12)
- "Where two or three gather in my name, there am I with them." (Matthew 18:20)

Pray together for deliverance
- "They cried out to [God] during the battle. He answered their prayers, because they trusted in him." (1 Chronicles 5:20)
- "Pray for each other so that you may be healed. The prayer of a righteous person is powerful and effective." (James 5:16)

(Include your own)
-
-

"The weapons we fight with are not the weapons of the world. On the contrary, they have divine power to demolish strongholds." (2 Corinthians 10:4)

Figure 9.3. Offensive spiritual weapons

NEXT STEP: ENVISION VICTORY

You wrote a realistic dialogue between you and your temptations. Now try writing one in which you put your battle plan into practice and overcome the enemy with God's truth and power. You can draw from your preventative, offensive, and defensive tactics, as well as truths about your redeemed self (identity statements) and any memorized verses.

Voice of Temptation	*Voice of Truth*

Tip: Try this exercise again after a few weeks and see how it changes. By repeating and practicing this exercise, you can track your progress as you grow in your ability to resist temptation.

A MOMENT TO PAUSE AND REFLECT

If you have made it this far in the curriculum, you've come a long way. Take a moment to look back on everything that has happened so far over the course of this group. Write down your responses to these two questions and then share them out loud:

How have you seen God at work in your life so far in this group?

In what areas of your sexuality would you like to see further healing and growth?

There may be times when you second-guess your progress and wonder if you have grown at all. Take heart: The journey of sexual freedom and healing is a life-long process, and the path is far from linear. In some ways, recovery never ends. This is bad news and good news: bad news because there is always more healing that needs to take place, but good news because there is always more healing available in Christ! Anyone who has been down this road can tell you that no matter how far we progress, we never graduate from the gospel. As one slogan puts it, "No matter how far down the road I travel, I'm just as close to the ditch." Our ongoing sin points us to God's ongoing grace.

Already, Jesus has freed us from the penalty of sin. Currently, he is freeing us from the power of sin. One day, he will free us from the very presence of sin. Yes we are free, and we are still being freed. Yes we have been healed, and we are still being healed. Sin is still in us, pointing us to Christ, thrusting us into his arms and keeping us close to the cross. The more we grow in awareness of our deep sin, the more we realize his deep love. The more we grow in awareness of God's deep love, the more we are able to face our sin. And best of all, the more we realize his love for us, the more we are able to truly love others, which is the entire purpose of our sexuality! We were made to love the way God loves. Our sexuality is designed to help us do that—to draw us into intimacy with God and other people.

There is no formula for spiritual warfare or sexual recovery. Because not everyone connects with God in the same way, not everyone should use the exact same methods. William Struthers offers this wisdom:

> As you go through recovery and healing, don't be afraid to let go of things that are not beneficial to you. If you find that journaling is tedious and stressful and increases your shame, stop doing it. If you find that listening to classical music soothes your soul and relieves work-related tension, listen to it. Because you have a unique personal history, you will have a unique path to recovery as well. Do not expect that what works for someone else must work with you. Do not expect that what doesn't work for someone else won't work for you either.

William Struthers, *Wired for Intimacy*

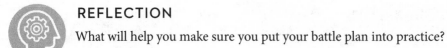

REFLECTION

What will help you make sure you put your battle plan into practice?

How is your prayer partner's battle plan different from yours?

THEME THREE

INTIMACY

10

HEALTHY INTIMACY

God created us for community and interdependence—
with him and with others. God is never alone. He is Trinity.
And we are created in his interdependent image.

ADELE AHLBERG CALHOUN, *SPIRITUAL DISCIPLINES HANDBOOK*

We are finally ready to move beyond breaking free from unhealthy sexual patterns and move toward pursuing sexual wholeness through healthy relationships. To thrive in God's kingdom no one *needs* sex, but *everyone* needs intimacy. After all, we were designed as sexual beings to express the love, intimacy, and joy God already enjoys as Trinity. In this session we'll talk about how we can meet our needs for close relationships in life-giving ways, which is the essence of healthy, thriving sexuality.

REVIEW. Think of a time when you felt especially close to someone—how did you feel? What is one word you would choose to describe that experience?

REFRAME. These words describe experiences of intimacy. Intimacy is not only something God gives to us, it is a central aspect of who God is. Christians believe God is relational at the core: Father, Son, and Holy Spirit, one God in three Persons. This means that God is inherently, incredibly intimate within himself. In fact, God *is* love (1 John 4:8). The words we used to describe what it's like to be especially close to someone describe *who God is.* This view of God is utterly

different than any view we could come up with on our own; it's too beautiful. And the implications are huge: who God is tells us who we are. We have been created in the relational image of the relational God. We were made for intimacy.

READ. Carefully read "Five Types of Intimacy" (p. 76).

REQUEST. Father, Son, and Holy Spirit, we love you. Thank you for giving us people to know and be known by, to love and be loved by. Take our desires for closeness and deepen them. Teach us how to satisfy our longings in healthy ways, until we relate to others as you have related to us. Amen.

FIVE TYPES OF INTIMACY

Sexuality is about so much more than having sex. Our sexuality plays a part in all human relationships, not just romantic ones. It not only includes sex acts but the entire experience of living as male or female sexual human beings.

Godly sexuality is ultimately about pursuing intimacy with God and others. We are not called to shut down our sexuality but to cultivate our sexual desires and longings in holy ways. The intimacy of being truly known and truly loved by another person has a healing effect on sexual brokenness. But in the absence of intimacy, isolation keeps us enslaved to sexual shame, loneliness, and despair. Pornography seduces us with the illusion of intimacy, while masturbation offers sexual stimulation apart from real relationships. Both threaten our ability to relate to the opposite sex in Christlike love. After all, our goal is not to just to avoid sinful lust but to grow in our capacity for loving, intimate relationships with real people.

Consider the following categories of intimacy:

Spiritual intimacy. No human bond can substitute for the spiritual intimacy of a love relationship with God. Yet even in the presence of God, we are not designed to function as isolated individuals. Spirituality cannot substitute for human contact. So while intimacy with God is an indispensable part of healing sexual brokenness, apart from strong relationships with others, it can only do so much.

Social intimacy. Social intimacy is what makes a close friendship close. It's the experience of knowing and being known, of loving and being loved. Social intimacy provides a sense of belonging to a person or a group of people. Evidence of strong social intimacy includes feeling accepted, significant, and secure.

This cannot happen overnight; it develops slowly, as trust is built over time.

Emotional intimacy. Emotional intimacy comes when we notice and process our feelings with another person. Too often, we ignore or invalidate our desires and disappointments, and try to cope with them on our own, sometimes through sexual outlets. We need to learn how to process our emotions together with others in life-giving ways that bring healing, not shame.

Mental intimacy. Mental/intellectual intimacy is closely tied to emotional intimacy. It means allowing someone to access your secret ideas, thoughts, and intentions. Mental intimacy exposes hidden thought patterns and lies, and invites the other person to listen and respond with truth.

Physical intimacy. Physical intimacy does not have to be erotic to be embodied. It can be as simple as a hug between friends.

INTIMACY NEEDS

Sexual brokenness is often the result of attempting to meet legitimate needs in unhealthy ways. Remember, we can survive and even thrive without sex, but we can't live according to God's design without intimacy. Intimacy is a need in the sense that we are hardwired for it. The point is not that we are entitled to it or that we always have to have it, but that we try to get it in all the wrong ways. Contemporary culture tells us the way to get real intimacy is through romance, and the way to avoid loneliness is through social media. Pornography combines the two; is it any wonder why so many of us are drawn to it? We have been conditioned to look for approval, acceptance, and affection where it cannot be found. We need to learn how to satisfy these legitimate longings in healthy ways.

Look at the following list of ten key intimacy needs. Circle the two or three that you desire most. Then answer how you have met these needs in unhealthy and healthy ways.

- comfort
- appreciation
- respect
- support
- acceptance
- approval
- encouragement
- affection
- attention
- security

How I have met these needs in unhealthy ways:

1.

2.

3.

How I can seek to meet these needs in healthy ways:

1.

2.

3.

Relational growth requires experience in real relationships; you can't develop intimacy in isolation. Use the following space to create a map of relationships in your life (see fig. 10.1 on p. 78). Include friends, family, mentors, and at least one member of your group.

1. Write your name in the oval.

2. Surrounding the oval, add names of friends, family members, mentors, and at least one member of your group.

3. Draw a line extending out to each person on the map.

4. As you review this relational map, select at least two people to cultivate deeper intimacy and interdependence with, including one member of your group. For each person, write one aspect of intimacy that relationship provides. Then choose one action step you will take to develop that relationship. (Action steps should be simple, healthy ways to cultivate relationships such as a weekly connection, a meal together, coffee, shared space, shared interests, a text, an email.)

-
-

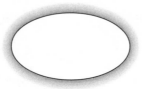

Figure 10.1. Map of relationships

Experts on sexuality acknowledge the necessity of strong relationships and authentic community for the development of healthy sexuality. This is why sexually broken people simply cannot experience healing in isolation: because our sexual desires are not really about sex at all. As Juli Slattery writes:

> Although we have hormones and sexual longings, they are not nearly as powerful as our drive for intimacy. The physical act of sex, while beautiful as an expression of intimacy, is a cheap replacement for it. We live in a world that sabotages intimacy at every step while promoting sex as an adequate substitute. No amount of sex (real or imagined) can compensate for a lack of intimacy.
>
> God may or may not have marriage for you in the future, but his will for you is to have intimate relationships within the body of Christ. In some cases, deep friendships can be even more fulfilling than marriage. David expressed this about his intimate friendship with Jonathan. Paul, who was single most (if not all of his life) shares in his writings about many intimate friendships who encouraged him through the years.
>
> Juli Slattery, "3 Ways You Can Be Sexual and Single"

NEXT STEP: INTIMACY SKILLS

Having an awareness of your need for intimate relationships is one thing; having the skills to cultivate them is another. This is an area where we can always improve—whether we are single, dating, or married. The more we learn how to be close to people in healthy, life-giving ways, the more we will experience our sexuality as a gift rather than a burden. Look at the various character qualities and skills that contribute to healthy relationships:

Identify two or three skills as your strengths.

Self-confidence	Service	Interdependence
Intentionality	Communication	Forgiveness
Trust	Empathy	Listening
Gentleness	Patience	Kindness
Honesty	Confession	Self-control
Prayer	Positive body image	Affirmation
Physical boundaries	Emotional boundaries	Letting go of control
Seeking wise counsel	Managing conflict	Spiritual boundaries
Caring for your own needs	Balancing work and play	Being fully present
Dedication to positive pursuits	Enjoying recreational activities	Acceptance of difficult feelings

Identify two or three skills where you wish to see growth.

Which of these skills do you see as most important for being married?

Which of these skills do you see as most important for being single?

Look back at the relationship map and the two individuals you selected.
For each of those relationships, choose one intimacy skill to practice with that person.
Use the following formula:
I will work on _____ with _____ by _____.

REFLECTION

What has God been teaching you about the concepts of sexuality and intimacy?

Which intimacy need or skill do you feel the need to focus on most, and why?

11

CHRISTLIKE SEXUALITY

*The Model of singleness par excellence—the figure who is
unmarried and best illustrates a life well lived—is Jesus.*

LAUREN WINNER, *REAL SEX*

Our goal as Christians is to become more Christlike in every area of life, including sexuality. But how can we imitate the sexuality of Jesus if Jesus never had sex? In what sense can we say that Jesus was sexual?

Christians believe that in the person of Jesus Christ, God became fully human. And in order to be human, he had to be sexual, with human sexual anatomy and desires. In the words of Gregory of Nazianzus, "that which he has not assumed, he has not redeemed." Unless Jesus is fully sexual, he is not fully our Savior. This language of Jesus being sexual sounds strange because many of us have inherited an underdeveloped theology of single sexuality. It's hard for us to understand how we can express our sexuality through singleness, and even harder to put it into practice.

Most of us would rather think of singleness as Jesus' calling rather than our own. He lived a single life until he died in his early thirties. Is this someone we really want to imitate? In reality, we are all single for significant periods of time. To become comfortable with the limits, constraints, and guidelines of singleness is to grow further into Christlikeness. But too often we see singleness not as a good gift from God, but as an unfortunate phase to endure on the way to marriage. Although we have often been taught to abstain from sex outside of marriage, we have not often been taught to embrace singleness as a unique way to enjoy life and connect with others.

REVIEW. What helpful or unhelpful messages about singleness have you heard?

REFRAME. As a single person, Jesus expressed his sexuality nonerotically. He cultivated intimate friendships with a select group of people. He didn't shy away from women like Mary and Martha; he also enjoyed connecting with their brother Lazarus. He loved people as he loved himself, putting their needs above his own, ultimately giving his life in exchange for theirs. In this way Jesus shows us the true purpose of sexuality: to embody the love of God. Although most of us will not be called to imitate his lifelong singleness, we all are called to imitate his attitude and heart.

READ. 1 John 4:7-12.

Dear friends, let us love one another, for love comes from God. Everyone who loves has been born of God and knows God. Whoever does not love does not know God, because God is love. This is how God showed his love among us: He sent his one and only Son into the world that we might live through him. This is love: not that we loved God, but that he loved us and sent his Son as an atoning sacrifice for our sins. Dear friends, since God so loved us, we also ought to love one another. No one has ever seen God; but if we love one another, God lives in us and his love is made complete in us.

REQUEST. Father, Son, and Holy Spirit, fill us with the mind and heart of Jesus Christ in our relationships. Let us embrace an others-oriented life, as if Jesus himself were the one living it. Come and use this time to minister your love to us and through us. Amen.

LUST VERSUS LOVE

Jesus was faced with the choice of what to do with his sexual desires—to love himself or to love others. We face this same choice in our daily lives, whether we single, dating, or married. Will we relate to other people selfishly out of lust or sacrificially out of love? The following exercise invites you to consider what Christlike sexuality can look like in different life situations.

Complete table 11.1 with examples of lustful versus loving (Christlike) approaches to sexuality.

Table 11.1. Lust versus love

THE SITUATION	LUSTFUL RESPONSES	LOVING RESPONSES
Singleness: You feel a strong desire for physical touch and affection. You wish you had someone to hold in this moment.		
Singleness: You've been spending a lot of time with someone you like. This person seems to like you back, even after recently going through a bad breakup.		
Dating: You realize the relationship you're in is no longer healthy. Still, you don't want it to end; you care a lot about this person.		
Dating: You just got engaged. You're wondering what physical and emotional boundaries would be wise to maintain at this stage.		
Marriage: You and your spouse find out you have significantly different sexual preferences.		
Marriage: You and your spouse get into an argument and feel bitter toward one another.		

According to Gary Thomas, many Christians struggling with sexual shame and sin "are focused on becoming unlike the devil rather than like Christ." Although Thomas specifically addresses addiction to pornography, his words apply just as much to other sexual struggles:

> Ultimately, victory over pornography will be enhanced when a person doesn't just focus on overcoming lust, but on becoming like Christ in all their attitudes and actions. This is a moment by moment decision over many things that have absolutely nothing to do with sex. When you practice humility and patience all day long, looking to serve others and put them first because that's what Christ would do, it seems out of character to then act like the devil late at night when you're by yourself. Train yourself in godliness throughout the day, and you'll likely find that the sin which had such a strong hold on you will lose much of its power and even, over time, much of its allure.

> Gary Thomas, "Slaying the Secret Sin"

NEXT STEP: SEXUAL INJUSTICE

Another way we can imitate Jesus in his approach to sexuality is by seeking justice for those who have been sexually exploited and abused. His mission to "set the oppressed free" (Luke 4:18) not only applies to those who are enslaved to viewing pornography but to those who are victims of the industry. Around the world, millions of women (and some men) live as victims of sex trafficking—an industry which feeds directly into the production of pornography. Because of this, viewing pornography not only damages the viewer; it perpetuates demand for modern-day sexual slave trade. When we take time to learn about this injustice, pray against it, and take action in small ways, we imitate Jesus and join him in his mission against evil.

Some facts.

- Trafficking women and children for sexual exploitation is the fastest growing criminal enterprise in the world, despite the fact that international law and the laws of 134 countries criminalize sex trafficking.

- At least 20.9 million adults and children are bought and sold worldwide into commercial sexual servitude, forced labor and bonded labor.

- About 2 million children are exploited every year in the global commercial sex trade.

- Almost 6 in 10 identified trafficking survivors were trafficked for sexual exploitation.

- Women and girls make up 98 percent of victims of trafficking for sexual exploitation.

Pray for justice. In response to these realities, take some time to pray together. Ask God to

1. open our eyes to the global sex industry

2. show us what role we play in the system

3. bring justice where there is sexual oppression

Pray together for

1. victims of sexual trafficking, exploitation, and abuse

2. perpetrators of sexual trafficking, exploitation, and abuse

3. producers of pornography fueling the global sex industry

4. participants in pornography fueling the global sex industry

5. consumers of pornography fueling the global sex industry

NOW WHAT?

To learn more about sexual injustice, consider watching the film *Nefarious: Merchant of Souls*. It's a documentary about sex trafficking that can challenge, disturb, and confront you. To get involved yourself, check out organizations such as International Justice Mission, Not for Sale, or Stop the Traffik. For more resources conveying the harmful effects of pornography, check out an organization called Fight the New Drug. Remember that every time we objectify other people—either by trafficking them or by looking at explicit pictures of them on the Internet—we deny their value as image bearers of God. But every time we seek justice for the marginalized and oppressed, we exhibit the image of Christ to a broken world.

REFLECTION

What implications does Jesus' sexuality have for your own sexuality?

In what ways are you challenged to become more like Christ?

12

PURSUING WHOLENESS

*God created us for intimate connection with him, with others,
and with ourselves. When those connections are broken or absent . . .
women desperately seek a false substitute. Sex or an intense
relationship offers the best stand-in for the real thing.*

MARNIE FERREE, *NO STONES*

Here we are—our final session. Some of you have reason to celebrate, since this experience has been transformative. Others may feel weary at this point—opening yourself up to this process has taken great courage and left you exhausted. For all of us, this journey has helped us embrace *vulnerability* by learning how to become transparent, *identity* by receiving God's truth, and *intimacy* by exploring Christlike ways to grow closer to others. Now it's time to take what you have learned in this group and put it into a vision of sexual wholeness for your own life.

REVIEW. What is one aspect of Christlike sexuality you are pursuing?

REFRAME. Some of us have begun to taste the freedom and victory of having our sexuality redeemed by Christ and renewed by the Holy Spirit. Others have trouble seeing any transformation, and we wonder if we'll ever progress beyond our current state. Ultimately, no matter how much or how little freedom and healing we've experienced, we can all look forward to the day when God returns and our sexuality will be fully healed.

READ. Revelation 21:1-7.

Then I saw "a new heaven and a new earth," for the first heaven and the first earth had passed away, and there was no longer any sea. I saw the Holy City, the new Jerusalem, coming down out of heaven from God, prepared as a bride beautifully dressed for her husband. And I heard a loud voice from the throne saying, "Look! God's dwelling place is now among the people, and he will dwell with them. They will be his people, and God himself will be with them and be their God. 'He will wipe every tear from their eyes. There will be no more death' or mourning or crying or pain, for the old order of things has passed away."

He who was seated on the throne said, "I am making everything new!" Then he said, "Write this down, for these words are trustworthy and true."

He said to me: "It is done. I am the Alpha and the Omega, the Beginning and the End. To the thirsty I will give water without cost from the spring of the water of life. Those who are victorious will inherit all this, and I will be their God and they will be my children."

REQUEST. Father, Son, and Holy Spirit, you are making all things new. Would you make us new too? Take our broken sexuality and make us whole, for your glory, for our joy, and for the good of the whole world. Amen.

SEXUAL WHOLENESS

As you may have learned by now, sexual brokenness is systemic. Because it affects every aspect of life, it requires a whole-life healing process. This process involves developing *spiritual intimacy* (in relation to God), a *supportive community* (in relation to others), a *secure identity* (in relation to self), *personal stewardship* (in relation to vocation), and a *healthy environment* (in relation to the world around us). When these ingredients come together, we experience sexuality as it was meant to be.

Just as sexual brokenness can be a result of nonsexual issues, sexual health can often arrive through nonsexual solutions. For example, people tend to sexually struggle less when spending quality time with God, close friends, or even simply by getting more sleep or more exercise. Making small changes to your daily routine can have enormous consequences, although you may not recognize them. Usually we are more aware of what is broken than what is healthy and strong. When our sexuality is broken, like a broken body part, it's hard not to think about it. When our sexuality is functioning properly, sometimes we don't even notice it!

On your own, take some time to evaluate your life for areas of brokenness, and then imagine how this area could become a place of health and wholeness. For each of the following categories, ask yourself (1) How is this area broken? and (2) What would healing look like for me? Then write your response after each of the five areas.

Relationship with God: *Spiritual intimacy*

   Examples

⊙ Reading, meditating on, and enjoying God's Word

⊙ Communing with God's presence in mundane activities

⊙ Keeping a gratitude journal to notice God at work in my life

Relationships with others: *Supportive community*

Examples

- ⦿ Spending time with someone who knows and loves me
- ⦿ Praying together regularly, especially through difficulties
- ⦿ Practicing confession and affirmation with a close friend

Relationship with myself: *Secure identity*

Examples

- ⦿ Accepting my identity in Christ and rejecting enemy accusations
- ⦿ Valuing my weaknesses as places where God can show his power
- ⦿ Taking holy pleasure in my body as a beautiful creation of God

Relationship with vocation: *Personal stewardship*

Examples

- ⦿ Faithfully working on the talents and tasks God has given me
- ⦿ Keeping rhythms of rest; practicing a form of sabbath
- ⦿ Taking time to bless others; leading my own small group

Systems of relationships: *A healthy environment*

Examples

- ⦿ Setting limits on the attention and energy I give to social media
- ⦿ Finding an older, wiser, trusted adult who is willing to mentor me
- ⦿ Following through on the actions I know I need to do to flourish

❯❯ NEXT STEP: SETTING GOALS

It's one thing to envision sexual wholeness; it's another to commit to the daily disciplines that make it a reality. Most likely, after leaving this group, your sexual recovery and health will either plateau or deteriorate if you don't have a strong system in place. What will it take to protect the progress you've made, and continue becoming more like Christ instead of going back to the person you used to be? As you leave this group, what are your goals?

Think S.M.A.R.T. It's important that these goals are Specific, Measurable, Achievable, Relevant, and Time-bound. Write one to three S.M.A.R.T. goals in the following space.

Example

I will find a mentor to support me after I leave this group (*specific*) who would be willing to meet with me weekly (*measurable*) who is an adult I know from school or church (*achievable*) in order to continue growing in sexual wholeness (*relevant*) by May 20, before I start work at my summer job (*time-bound*).

1.

2.

3.

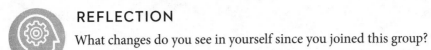

REFLECTION

What changes do you see in yourself since you joined this group?

What was the most important thing you learned?

ACKNOWLEDGMENTS

This curriculum began as a creative project at Wheaton College Graduate School. It was supervised by David Setran and Dan Haase whose influence cannot be measured. Training in dialogue education shaped the curriculum's design, namely through an intensive class facilitated by Jeanette Romkema through Global Learning Partners.

Thanks to those who provided critical support along the way: Sandy and Yvonne Boa prayed consistently and gave generously to make this project possible; Michael Tso saw its potential before I did and challenged me to trust God at every point; Skye Jethani and David Sanford helped me enter the world of Christian publishing.

Thanks to Luke Miller, Cindy Bunch, and Elissa Schauer at IVP for recognizing the value of this work. Elissa, my editor, sharpened my writing and refined this resource into something more powerful and usable than I ever could have produced on my own.

Thanks to many students at Wheaton College whose feedback led to a number of improvements. Women's leaders pointed out gender bias at various points and made this resource more suitable for women's groups.

Most of all, thanks to the prayer partners who have supported me in my own healing journey: Andrew Thompson, Adam Callaway, Daniel Cummings, Zack Smiley, Bill Hood, Roman Czerwinski, Corbin Renken, Ben Bergstrom, Daniel MacLachlan, Hezekiah Franklin, Pete Rizzo, and now my wife, Rebecca Boa. You accepted me, gospeled me, and prayed for me when I needed it most. Thank you for connecting me to the healing presence and transforming power of God.

HOW TO CHECK IN

Many groups set aside time for checking in without a clear criteria for how to do this well. In a sexual support group, updates often become either stagnant or stressful. Either people feel closer and more connected but nothing really changes (stagnant), or they feel the need to change but also more pressure as a result (stressful). The solution is *not* to stop checking in with each other. We can't dismiss the importance of staying in touch with the people in our group (especially our prayer partners); instead, we need to be intentional about how we do it.

People usually check in (1) at the beginning of group meetings, or (2) during weekly time with prayer partners.

The following is a simple structure you can follow with your group or with your prayer partner:

1. Share one word to describe how you have been feeling lately.

2. Succinctly explain how you have been doing sexually and why.

3. Conclude your update with one of the following statements:

   - I would like to be encouraged.

   - I would like to be challenged.

   - I would like to be encouraged *and* challenged.

   - I'll pass.

If you are doing this with your prayer partner, follow up by praying for one another.

Ideally, check ins are

- *Transparent, but not too long.* Authentic sharing takes time. But especially in a large group, updates can take up the majority of a meeting if left without limits.

- *Short, but not shallow.* If check ins *are* kept short, it might be difficult to go below the surface level. Think of an update as a summary of recent events and emotions.

○ *Safe, not stressful.* Fully listen to each person giving an update. Let your attention be an act of love and acceptance. Don't let people give advice during this time.

○ *Encouraging, not excusing.* If the person giving an update would like to be encouraged, give encouragement. Notice signs of improvement. Don't excuse bad behavior. Communicate the gospel and apply it to the person's life situation.

- *Example:* "I appreciate how you have been reaching out when you're feeling tempted. Thanks for setting an example of courage and humility to admit when you need help."

○ *Challenging, not comfortable.* If the person giving an update would like to be challenged, offer a challenge. Make sure the challenge is both doable and measurable so you can follow up. Give the person permission to accept or reject your challenge.

- *Example:* "You mentioned how staying up late has been a trigger for you to act out. What if you commit to going to bed by 11 p.m. every night this week?"

PRAYERS FOR THE JOURNEY

If your group is so inclined, you can use these prayers to open a weekly meeting. Alternatively, you can use the prayers on this page to open the weekly meeting, and those on the next page to close it.

Prayer of Confession

Christ the light of the world has come to dispel the darkness of our hearts.

In his light let us examine ourselves and confess our sins.

(Silence is kept)

Lord of grace and truth, we confess our unworthiness to stand in your presence as your children.

We have sinned: forgive and heal us.

We have lived by our own strength,

and not by the power of your resurrection.

In your mercy, forgive us.

All   **Lord, hear us and help us.**

We have lived by the light of our own eyes,

as faithless and not believing.

In your mercy, forgive us.

All   **Lord, hear us and help us.**

We have lived for this world alone,

and doubted our home in heaven.

In your mercy, forgive us.

All   **Lord, hear us and help us.**

Most merciful God,

we confess that we have sinned against you

in thought, word, and deed,

by what we have done,

and by what we have left undone.

We have not loved you with our whole heart;

we have not loved our neighbors as ourselves.

We are truly sorry and we humbly repent.

For the sake of your Son Jesus Christ,

have mercy on us and forgive us;

that we may delight in your will,

and walk in your ways,

to the glory of your Name. Amen.

Prayer of Deliverance

O Lord, arise, help us, and deliver us for thy Name's sake,
through Jesus Christ our Lord; who was tempted in every
way as we are, yet did not sin. By his grace we are able to
triumph over every evil, and to live no longer for ourselves
alone, but for him who died for us and rose again. Amen.

Prayer of Assurance

May the God of all healing and forgiveness
draw us to himself,
and cleanse us from all our sins
that we may behold the glory of his Son,
Jesus Christ our Lord.

All   **Amen.**

May the Father of all mercies,
who sent his Son into the world to save sinners,
bring us his pardon and peace, now and forever,
to the praise and glory of his name.

All   **Amen.**

Eternal God, heavenly Father,

you have graciously accepted us as living members

of your Son our Savior Jesus Christ.

Send us now into the world in peace,

and grant us strength and courage

to love and serve you

with gladness and singleness of heart;

through Christ our Lord. Amen.

Prayer of Blessing

All our problems of this life on earth

All   **We send to the Cross of Christ.**

All the difficulties of our circumstances

All   **We send to the Cross of Christ.**

All the devil's works from his temporary power

All   **We send to the Cross of Christ.**

All our hopes for wholeness and eternal life

All   **We set on the risen Christ.**

Christ the Sun of Righteousness shine upon us

and scatter the darkness from before our path,

and the blessings of God Almighty, Father, Son and Holy Spirit,

be among us and remain with us always. Amen.

TIPS FOR JOURNALING

Journaling allows us to slow down and process what God is doing in our own lives. Journaling also reminds us that what happens *outside* of group meetings matters more than what happens *inside* group meetings. While journaling is not for everyone, it can be a great tool so don't be afraid to at least try it.

FIVE TIPS FOR JOURNALING

Don't track the negatives. Participants often use journals to track their progress by "counting the days" since giving in to sexual temptation and acting out. Because this measures a surface-level indicator, it can promote a legalistic mindset, resulting either in pride and self-righteousness or shame and discouragement. If you do keep track of your behavior, make it an occasion to praise God for periods of sobriety, and a reminder to return to him after slips or relapses.

Track positive connections. Instead of keeping track of your sexual behavior, try keeping track of your times in prayer with others outside of group meetings. This puts the focus on seeking God together on a regular basis instead of dwelling on individual successes or failures. Tracking the frequency of your times in prayer with others promotes interdependence and consistent contact in gospel-focused friendships.

Process and pray through what you are learning. Journaling is a great way to reflect on how God might be teaching, leading, and transforming you throughout your group experience. Your journal can become a place of prayer and intimacy with God through the ups and downs of your journey to sexual wholeness. The journal prompts attached to each session are meant to serve as starting points for this good work of reflection.

Do what works for you. There is no right or wrong way to journal. If you're having trouble, try different ways of journaling: making lists, writing poems, drawing pictures, meditating on Scripture passages, and so on. Whatever helps you connect with God and process your experiences, do it. Whatever doesn't help you, don't do it.

Share it with someone else. Try sharing the key points of your journal with your prayer partner(s). This will enhance your relationship, your ability to articulate what you have been learning, and your motivation to put words into action.

LEADER'S NOTES

LEADERSHIP QUALIFICATIONS

Redeemed Sexuality is designed to accommodate peer-to-peer leadership. Granted, certain qualifications are necessary in order for your leadership to be effective:

1. Leaders must be followers of Jesus Christ and at least eighteen years old (preferably older).

2. Leaders must be actively growing in their own personal journeys of sexual discipleship.

3. Leaders must be able to devote time and energy to this group outside of group meetings.

4. Leaders must be ready to adapt and modify the curriculum based on their group's needs.

5. Leaders must be willing to demonstrate deep vulnerability to the people in their group.

HOW TO LEAD A REDEEMED GROUP

1. Ask for prayer support from people who are close to you.

2. Pray for the Holy Spirit to lead you as you lead others.

3. Assemble a group of four to eight Christians of your same gender.

4. Check in with potential participants before your first meeting.

5. Have each person read and sign the Group Covenant (p. 9).

6. Use *Redeemed Sexuality* as the basic structure for your group.

7. Invite a friend or mentor to actively support you as a leader.

8. Be prepared to share your sexual history at the first meeting. (See guidelines on pp. 17-19.)

9. Gather for ninety minutes once a week as long as the group lasts.

10. Create a "closing ceremony" to conclude each weekly gathering.

11. Partner people up to pray with one another throughout the week.

Be sure to take step one seriously, and ask for prayer support from people who are close to you. Leading a group means taking a stand against the enemy, which makes you especially vulnerable. You absolutely need to have people praying for you, both for the sake of your group and for your own spiritual health. *Tip:* Grandmothers are particularly diligent in praying for any grandchild who needs help against sexual shame or pornography! Seriously.

NOTES ON THE LEADER'S NOTES

◉ Before each of the three groups of sessions or themes (Vulnerability, Identity, and Intimacy) you will find a "Theme Page" introducing that section of the curriculum. Reading the theme pages in advance will help you learn a little bit about the content yourself before leading others through it.

◉ Each page of leader's notes on a specific session includes a summary of the session's purpose, helpful tips you can use, challenges you will face, and recommended resources on the subject.

◉ The last point of each "Helpful Tips" section provides an illustration of the main theme for the session. These illustrations help to clarify the overall point of the session, especially for those who think less analytically and more imaginatively. If you find an illustration helpful, you can pass it on to your group.

THEME ONE: VULNERABILITY

So you want to lead a Redeemed group. Are *you* willing to be vulnerable? To be uncomfortable? To be seen and known as you actually are, not as you should be? If the answer to these questions is yes, then you're ready to help this group do some difficult soul work. Growing in vulnerability is tough.

In this curriculum, one of the first steps is having each person share their story with your group. The second step is exploring the most painful and difficult parts of that story. The third step is identifying the lies underneath sexual struggles and replacing them with truth. The fourth step is learning to practice confession and affirmation.

This theme of the curriculum breaks us down before it builds us up. Session 1 introduces new and challenging concepts. Sessions 2 and 3 require a lot of emotional energy. Thankfully, sessions 4 and 5 offer a change of pace by introducing practical tools for the journey to sexual health and freedom. If we stay with the process, even when it's painful, we will avoid settling for shallow solutions and emerge with a deeper experience of healing. Deeper relationships will also be formed as we go through the gauntlet of letting our guard down together.

Vulnerability allows the hidden, unwanted, and even ugly aspects of oneself to be known by others. It not only involves exposing our hearts to others but allowing them to minister to us. Vulnerability plays an essential role in developing sexual wholeness by opening up the door to real—not fake—relationships. Here are three tips to offer group members that can increase the level of vulnerability in the group.

◉ *Lead the way.* If you want to see vulnerability, be the chief repenter of your group— the one who is most aware of your own sin and most in need of God's grace on a daily basis (1 Timothy 1:15). This doesn't mean you should grovel in guilt. Neither should you contrive confessions if you can't think of anything. It *does* mean you need to be keenly aware of your own weaknesses and temptations, and the lies that you are prone to believing. And you need to be open about them. Here's what you can expect: people in your group will tend to be less vulnerable with you than you are with them. So you need to go *deep*. The more honest you are about your shame and brokenness, the more freedom others will feel to stop posing, stop pretending, and be real. Vulnerability starts with you.

○ *Practice during the week.* If confession is only done during group meetings, it will probably become either a weekly dump, in which group members seek to feel better about their failures, or a weekly checkup, in which group members feel obligated to report their performance. This is why many groups end up stagnating after a few weeks of antilust updates. In meetings, confession tends to stay on the surface and behavior focused. It either makes people feel stressed out because of their failures or superior because of their success. Participants often find themselves able to reach a deeper level of vulnerability with a prayer partner during the week than with the entire group during weekly meetings. For a simple structure to use for checking in with one another (either as prayer partners or as a group), see appendix 1.

○ *Do not only confess your sins.* Confess your thoughts, temptations, feelings, struggles, idols, insecurities. These are not sins, but they're still difficult to talk about—especially when you're in the middle of them. Confessing thoughts and emotions allows us to get below the surface to talk about *why* we are struggling, so that we can actually begin to change. Shallow, abstract confessions like "I fell" or "I messed up" transform no one. Deeper confession paves the way to deeper vulnerability.

Session 1. Learning the Language

Purpose: To familiarize everyone with basic sexual terminology and language to use in the group.

Helpful tips. Before each weekly gathering, read through the session and its leader's notes. In this session's main activity, "A Common Vocabulary," don't try to read the entire document together with the group. Instead, give them a few minutes to look over the vocabulary, and then point out significant terms for discussion. If participants want to read it all, they can do so on their own. Whatever you don't get to talk about can provide interesting topics for future conversations.

If possible, share your story with the group at the end of this first meeting. This will set a standard of vulnerability and minimize the time it will take for everyone to share their stories next time. By sharing your story first, you create a group dynamic that is *safe but not comfortable.* Work through "Next Step: Preparing Your Story" before you share. Go deeper than what is comfortable for you; it's always terrifying, but it's worth it. When you share your darkest sexual secrets, God's power will be made perfect in your weakness! By doing so, you can inspire participants to go deeper than they ever planned or expected to go. People may even share things they have never told anyone before—or realized themselves. This is extremely special; it means they are taking the first step to freedom.

Have your group download onto their smart phones a social recovery app called "rTribe." Using rTribe allows group members to communicate more effectively and offer support to each other throughout the week. rTribe includes helpful features like the "I'm Triggered" button, which reaches out to everyone in your group to notify them that you could use help at that moment.

Some group leaders find their weekly meetings enhanced by singing. Worship songs can be so powerful in a group like this, where everyone is highly aware of their need for Christ. Especially if your group is musically inclined, try singing together and see how it goes.

Every group is unique, so whether you have led multiple groups or this is your first time, there are many ways you can grow as a leader. So after each meeting, ask yourself or your co-leader these three questions: (1) What worked well? (2) What didn't work well? (3) What could I or we do differently?

Challenges. It will most likely take a while for participants to start using the language introduced by "A Common Vocabulary." They might return to euphemisms like "I messed up" instead of clinical language to describe times of sexually acting out. You'll need to discern how to address this as it comes up. Asking someone to use different terminology during a meeting can come off as judgmental. At the same time, participants need to get used to talking about sexuality in a more mature way. You can help them do this by modeling it yourself. The more you use a mature vocabulary, over time you'll notice participants using the same language you use.

Remind people to finish "Next Step: Preparing Your Story" before your next gathering. It can only be completed individually and takes a while to process. In fact, it can be helpful for participants to start working through their sexual histories before the group starts meeting at all! Besides connecting regularly with a prayer partner, this is the only exercise of *Redeemed Sexuality* that participants complete outside of weekly meetings.

Recommended Resources

For men

- *Wired for Intimacy: How Pornography Hijacks the Male Brain* by William Struthers

- *Pure Desire: How One Man's Triumph Can Help Others Break Free* by Ted Roberts

- *Finally Free: Fighting for Purity with the Power of Grace* by Heath Lambert

For women

- *No Stones: Women Redeemed from Sexual Addiction* by Marnie Ferree

- *Beggar's Daughter: From the Rags of Pornography to the Riches of Grace* by Jessica Harris

- *Real Sex: The Naked Truth About Chastity* by Lauren Winner

For everyone

- *Closing the Window: Steps to Living Porn Free* by Tim Chester

- *Healing the Wounds of Sexual Addiction* by Mark Laaser

- *Sex Is Not the Problem (Lust Is)* by Joshua Harris

- *How Pornography Harms* by John Foubert

Session 2. Telling Your Story

Purpose: To review our sexual histories in-depth, tell our stories out loud, and pray for each other.

Helpful tips. You never know what someone will share, and you might not know what to say. No matter how deep or dark the story is, it's never a bad idea to respond with a simple "Thank you." If you hear an especially difficult story, consider whether the person might need more help than the group can provide. Mental illnesses, experiences of sexual abuse, and severe sexual addictions fall into this category. If you suspect someone in your group is dealing with one or more of these issues, don't hesitate to refer that person to a trained professional.

If even only one person can't attend the main activity, "Sharing Stories," reschedule it. And afterwards, don't let any more participants into the group. Either you will waste time trying to catch them up or you will violate the principle of safety by having some people know more about each other than others. Adding new members after "Sharing Stories" irreversibly damages the group dynamic you are trying to create.

Make sure everyone completes "Next Step: Prayer Partners," even if it's not during a weekly meeting. As long as you explain the exercise, it should not require facilitation from a leader.

Sharing your sexual history is like giving someone a tour of your home. We like to make sure our homes are clean and visually pleasing before showing them to visitors. Sometimes we do a surface-level sweep, stuffing messy clutter and dirty laundry into a closet where it won't be seen. However, this is *not* the goal of sharing your sexual history. The goal of giving someone a tour of your sexual history is not to hide the mess or the dirty stains, but to expose them in the presence of people you can trust. Perhaps there is a dark corner of your story where there is no light. Perhaps there is a stench coming from a dirty closet that you

don't want to open up. Maybe you've never shown what's inside to anyone before. It's time go into that dark place, turn on the light, and let the vulnerability begin.

Challenges. "Sharing Stories" tends to go much longer than anticipated. If your group is not able to find one or two extended time slots to complete it, it can end up taking a month's worth of weekly meetings just to get through everyone's stories. Expect it to take longer than you think, and for good reason: for some, sharing stories is the most important and powerful part of the healing process.

While listening to the stories of others, people get tired. Make sure food, drinks, and snacks are provided to help everyone pay attention. Take a short break after every story.

Recommended Resources

◉ Audrey Assad's testimony:
   soundcloud.com/udreyssad/personal-witness

◉ Nate Larkin's testimony:
   www.iamsecond.com/seconds/nate-larkin

Session 3. Wounds of the Past

Purpose: To face any unresolved wounds related to present sexual struggles, and begin the process of forgiving.

Helpful tips. After completing the main activity, "Forgiveness," remind participants that they have finished the longest and most difficult sessions of the curriculum. Now that they have acknowledged their sexual past and pain to one another, they can start looking at the heart of their present sexual struggles.

In "Next Step: Family Issues," the goal is not necessarily to decide which statements about sex reflect healthy, biblical attitudes, but to dialogue about how these attitudes affect us. You might try asking which statements people think are most common, the most destructive, or the most helpful.

As a leader, your job is not to counsel participants but to create a supportive space for them to engage the healing process. For those whose wounds are more severe, you can direct them to seek professional help from a counselor. This doesn't mean they have to leave your group but that the hard issues they are dealing with require more support than peers or small group leaders alone are able to offer.

Forgiving those who have wounded us is like healing from a burn. It will require surgery—maybe even multiple surgeries. The doctor will cut open the skin of the patient in order to access the place where work will be done. In order for healing to take place, a new incision must be made. But unlike at the hospital, there is no anesthetic to knock us unconscious. When Jesus the master Physician performs surgery, his patients are wide awake. He does it this way because our bodies not only need healing but our souls as well. Some burns require you to pop your blisters and scrub away the dead skin around the burn area every day. In the same way, forgiving others is a process; it takes surgery, and it takes time, as bitterness pops up again and again. Let Jesus do his work, and give yourself grace in the process; forgiveness is not a one-time event.

Challenges. The "Forgiveness" section can feel heavy because it contains emotionally difficult content. People in your group may feel drained by it, especially after telling their stories the previous week. You can encourage them with the assurance that future sessions will get easier, and that we need to do this hard work of going through our pasts while our stories are fresh on our minds. The pain of facing wounds of the past makes this session arguably the most difficult of all.

If you think this session might be too heavy or too soon for your group, then consider skipping it and coming back to it at a later point. Remember that this curriculum is not intended to be followed rigidly, but to be adapted to the needs of participants and modified as you see fit.

Recommended Resources

- *Rid of My Disgrace: Hope and Healing for Victims of Sexual Assault* by Justin Holcomb and Lindsey Holcomb

- *Healing the Wounds of Sexual Addiction* (chaps. 7–8) by Mark Laaser

Session 4. Truth and Lies

Purpose: To expose roots of sexual brokenness, and replace lies with truths from God's Word.

Helpful tips. In the main activity, "Leaves and Roots," read either "Ashley's Story" or "Tom's Story" out loud as a group, switching the reader at each numbered point. This will help everyone pay attention, notice the details of the story, and grow more comfortable in talking about sexuality.

Use "Next Step: Memorization" as a launch pad for continued practice. Even memorizing one verse per week can strengthen and renew our minds. Meditating on a bite-sized verse during the day can crowd out the selfish sexual thinking that often dominates our brains by default. Without God's Word to deliver us, we cannot overcome the lies behind sexual temptation. Make memorization a small, steady habit in your day. Think of it as wallpapering your mind with beauty rather than cheap posters.

If you want to remove a weed, you have to dig down to the roots. You can try to chop away at the leaves of your sins all day and never touch the lies at the heart of them. If you don't dig up the roots, they will grow back even stronger than before. To make progress in pulling weeds of sexual sin, we must learn to carefully remove the deeper roots out of our thought life and replace each buried lie with a new seed that will bear good fruit—truth from the word of God.

Challenges. Most participants are more comfortable talking about sexual surface symptoms (like masturbation and pornography) than deeper issues (thought patterns and difficult emotions). This session challenges them to talk about what's actually going on in their brains. As multiple authors have noted, the largest and most powerful sexual organ in the human body is actually the brain. When brains are transformed, behavior will follow. Participants need to start realizing and replacing lies in their lives with the truth of God's Word *now*, not later. If their brains don't change, not much else will.

People may notice that "Tom's Story" and "Ashley's Story" follow the same basic structure, and contain only slight variations. On the one hand, this might appear to be an oversimplification of the differences between how men and women experience sexual addiction. On the other hand, for the sake of initiating discussion, only a narrow range of experiences could be represented in the case studies. The point of the stories is to start a conversation. Participants can use these narratives to talk about how we tend to fall into sexual shame and sin, and how we can avoid and overcome it. The stories can even be used to discuss how to minister to others who find themselves in similar situations.

Recommended Reading

- *Victory over the Darkness* by Neil T. Anderson
- *Winning the Battle Within* by Neil T. Anderson

Session 5. Confession

Purpose: To learn principles and practices of effective confession and affirmation.

Helpful tips. Remember, your job as the leader is to be the chief repenter of your group. Re-read "Lead the Way" on page 100-101 to review how to be help your group increase in vulnerability.

Beware of practicing confession to the exclusion of practicing affirmation. "Next Step: Practicing Affirmation" can help with that. Too much confession without affirmation leads to despair, because people start to doubt that they are making real progress. Too much affirmation without confession leads to complacency, because people begin to feel nonchalant about their sins. So create a group culture of both confession *and* affirmation (see appendix 1). Try taking some time for affirmation at the end of each session. Affirmation completes confession; along with confessing the darkness of sin we see in our own hearts, we affirm the light of Christ we see in one another!

Practicing confession and affirmation together is like spiritual breathing. When we confess to one another, we spiritually exhale the toxins that would slowly eat us alive if we kept them buried inside. When we affirm one another, we spiritually inhale words of truth and love that fill us up like fresh air and build our confidence. Don't stop breathing! May the winds of honest confession and heartfelt affirmation blow through the atmosphere of your group.

Challenges. Confession in sexual support groups can be shallow, repetitive, and ultimately unhelpful. This is often the case when confessions only happen *after* sexually acting out, not before or during struggles and temptations. Too often, people use confession either as an emotional dump to make themselves feel better afterward or as sin management to monitor the frequency of their bad behavior. The main activity, "Effective Confession," will help your group learn how to do confession well, so that it leads to transformation, not frustration or stagnation. When done right, confession opens the door to incredible spiritual growth as people repent and return to the Lord.

When groups do succeed at practicing deep confession, it can eat up the majority of a weekly meeting if it lacks structure. See appendix 1 for a structure you can use to make group confessions transparent, but not too long, and complemented by words of affirmation.

Recommended Reading

◉ "Confession and Communion" in *Life Together* by Dietrich Bonhoeffer

◉ *Practicing Affirmation: God-Centered Praise of Those Who Are Not God* by Sam Crabtree

THEME TWO: IDENTITY

In this curriculum, *identity* refers to a person's fundamental sense of self: the inner source of value, security, and significance. Identity is a person's center of making meaning, motivating all action, including sexual behavior. *Identity in Christ* refers to a sense of self that is grounded in the person and work of Jesus Christ. Identity in Christ fuels sexual health by providing inner resources needed to overcome sexual brokenness.

Cycles of sexual sin and shame begin with the *wounded self*—a broken sense of identity—which triggers shame-based thought patterns and unhealthy sexual behaviors that then lead to despair (reinforcing and ultimately restarting the cycle). But if we are able to disrupt the narrative of the wounded self, we begin to break the cycle. This is the goal of the next few sessions: to deconstruct the wounded self in exchange for the reality of the *redeemed self*. Cycles of sexual freedom and healing are rooted in the redeemed self—a renewed sense of identity in Christ. When the gospel is telling us who we are, it changes what we do by initiating worship and life-giving habits that lead to true fulfillment in loving God and others

(reinforcing this new cycle). While the shape of these cycles look different for every person, the core issue of identity remains the same.

The gospel actually rearranges the concept of sexual identity. Instead of having sexual preferences as the basis of who we are, who we are *in Christ* serves as the basis of our sexuality. Instead of a self-centered identity that says, "My sexual preferences define who I am," a Christ-centered identity says, "Who I am defines my sexual priorities." Identity in Christ—being loved by the Father, saved by Jesus, made new by the Holy Spirit—becomes the foundation of a redemptive approach to sexuality.

Because of this, *Redeemed Sexuality* it is not mainly about studying the Bible. It's about rediscovering the power of our gospel-given identity and using the Word of God as a weapon of spiritual warfare toward this goal. It's about exposing lies we believe that keep us in sexual bondage and countering them with the truth of who we are in Christ. As Jesus said, "The truth will set you free" (John 8:32).

We don't seek truth simply by finding out what God tells us to do. For some people, this only reinforces the cycle of guilt and shame. Instead, we read the Bible to gain a clearer vision of who Jesus is, what he did, and the extraordinary implications of his death and resurrection.

Perhaps the most important implication is what the Bible tells us about our identity; namely, that we are beloved sons and daughters of the most high King. When we fully accept this belovedness as the truest thing about us, and realize that we are seen as infinitely desirable in the eyes of the Creator and Redeemer of the universe, then sexual shame and sin have no place in our lives.

For people to break the cycle of shame and heal from addiction, it is not enough to simply analyze Scripture and motivate ourselves to obey its commands. We must move beyond accumulating knowledge and tinkering with spiritual disciplines and learn to behold the beauty of the risen Christ. Only when we have been captured by a ravishing vision of Jesus and our identity in him can we genuinely accept his invitation to take over every area of our lives—including our sexuality.

Session 6. The Wounded Self

Purpose: To understand how broken self-image fuels cycles of sexual brokenness and redemption.

Helpful tips. Pay attention to the insights that emerge during the main activity, "Cycles of Sexual Behavior." Participants may realize key information about their core beliefs or cycles of behavior that will shed light on what lies behind their sexual struggles. They will also use the "cycle of redemption" (fig. 6.2) to imagine what it will take for them to initiate and sustain a lifestyle of Christlike sexuality. There is therefore a practical side to this exercise: figuring out what will help

each person break free from sources of sexual brokenness and start pursuing personal patterns of spiritual growth.

Here's why "Next Step: Healthy Body Image" matters: self-image affects sexual behavior like the exterior of a building affects vandalism. A newly built building is rarely vandalized, but if a few windows break, it becomes a target for graffiti. As long as it is seen as beautiful and worthy (especially by the owner), it will be treated as such. However, when abandoned or devalued, it will be used however people want to use it. How we see ourselves affects the way we treat our bodies and those of others: as beautiful works of art to be celebrated and protected or as open targets to be used and acted upon. Ultimately, "Healthy Body Image" is designed to promote attitudes of acceptance, gratitude, and stewardship in regard to our bodies, which (though fallen) God has created as good.

If you do decide to complete "Positive Body Image," try creating a culture of verbal encouragement and affirmation of physical appearance. Complementing one another on what we wear or how we look can build confidence and confront the wounded self. Appreciating our physical bodies is one way to affirm our identity as being created in the image of God, as well as our identity as being redeemed in that same image.

Challenges. In "Cycles of Sexual Behavior," people who don't identify as sexual addicts might not think the cycle of addiction is for them. In reality, the cycle represents dynamics of shame and sin common to every person, exaggerated in people whose behavior has become totally unmanageable. You don't have to be an addict to find yourself in the cycle, and you don't have to specifically struggle with masturbation or pornography to get stuck in it. Participants may need to modify the cycles in order to more accurately represent their own patterns of behavior. The point is to visualize and understand how easy it is to find ourselves trapped by sexual shame and sin, and how we can find a way to freedom through Christ.

"Healthy Body Image" may prove to be an uncomfortable and even shame-inducing exercise. Especially if you're leading a women's group, discern whether or not everyone in your group is ready to talk about their bodies and willing to participate fully. Tread lightly; this topic is delicate and potentially scary precisely because it's so important.

Recommended Reading

- ⦿ *Out of the Shadows* and *Facing the Shadow* by Patrick Carnes

- ⦿ *L.I.F.E. Recovery Guides* by Mark Laaser and Marnie Ferree

- ⦿ *Making Advances: A Comprehensive Guide for Treating Female Sex and Love Addicts* by Marnie Ferree

Session 7. Identity in Christ

Purpose: To attune ourselves to the voice of Jesus and discover the power of who we are in Christ.

Helpful tips. This is the only session with two main activities: "The Double Lie" and "Who Am I in Christ?" Both activities are short yet powerful. Make sure to complete both. The truths of "Who Am I in Christ?" create the foundation for spiritual and sexual wholeness. Groups come back to the identity statements again and again to remind themselves of these core truths. They transform the way we see ourselves, lifting us out of self-centered thinking and onto the cycle of redemption.

In "Who Am I in Christ?" take note of which identity statement each participant resonates with the most. You can use it to encourage them later on. Some leaders purchase individualized bracelets with identity statements on them for participants to keep as a memory of the group and of their identity in Christ. Encourage group members to write down a few of the statements (or the entire list) and then post them on their bedroom or bathroom walls to read in the mornings and evenings. This session may be the most important one of all; unless participants begin to grasp the truth of their identity in Christ, they'll never move beyond behavior modification into deep transformation.

As your group works through the identity theme, take a minute or two at the end of each weekly meeting to read a few identity statements out loud before closing. This may seem repetitive, but it models for them how to reinforce these truths until they become engrained into participants' brains.

When we reclaim our identity in Christ, we look at ourselves though the eyes of a restoration artist, the God who loves us and makes us new. Seeing treasure beneath trash, a restorer buys something damaged, owns it, and works on it until it fully becomes what he intends it to be. Sometimes, when we sexually act out, we feel like we have undone God's work of restoration. So we despair over our broken condition. We need to learn to see ourselves as God sees us. God is restoring his Son's image in us. He is the ultimate restoration artist, and he specializes in brokenness. Where we see wreckage, he sees a masterpiece in the making.

Challenges. The section titled "Who Are We in Christ?" balances out the individualism of the other identity statements. God does not only save us as individuals but as the community of believers we are united with. We cannot separate our status as God's beloved sons and daughters from our relationships and responsibilities to one another as sisters and brothers.

In "Next Step: The Voice of Jesus," you may wonder which passage to choose to read with your group. The first two passages (John 8; Luke 7) take a more imaginative approach. The third (Romans 5–8) takes a more intellectual approach. Since the point is to read a Bible passage that connects the love of Christ to sexual shame and sin, choose whichever one feels most natural for you. If none of these options appeal to you, feel free to use a biblical text of your own choosing.

Recommended Reading

◎ *Who Am I? Identity in Christ* by Jerry Bridges

◎ *Who Do You Think You Are?* by Mark Driscoll

Session 8. Facing Temptation

Purpose: To identify personal triggers and explore dynamics of sexual temptation.

Helpful tips. It's often helpful for participants to practice the main activity, "Temptation Dialogue," on their own as a way to improve their ability to overcome the temptations they face. Over time, they become more aware of repeated patterns and less susceptible to the same old strategies that used to defeat them every time.

For "Next Step: Legalism and License," it might be good to explain the difference between healthy and legalistic approaches to keeping track of progress in sexual recovery. On the one hand, noting how long it's been since you last sexually acted out can be a celebration of sobriety and growth. On the other hand, it can be an occasion for self-righteous pride and even despair if you lose your "streak." Remember that the number of days since you sexually acted out is only a surface indicator of change, and cannot measure the transformation that God is working in your heart.

Temptation can feel like a court battle in which we are the defendants. At times we act like attorneys trying to defend ourselves against the lies of the accuser. Other times, when we know we have broken the law, we become our own accusers. In the court of temptation, we often forget that "we have an advocate with the Father—Jesus Christ, the Righteous One" (1 John 2:1). We have a top-tier lawyer with an infallible case, and he does the talking. We don't need to address the voices of accusation ourselves but can politely refer them to the one who speaks on our behalf. After all, not even Jesus used his own power to defend himself against temptation, but depended on the strength of God's Word for his deliverance. In battle, he let "the sword of the Spirit, which is the word of God" do the talking.

Challenges. "Temptation Dialogue" can challenge and even frighten participants because it involves getting in the enemy's head and coming face-to-face with the darkness within. People can be disturbed by realizing the thoughts running through their heads during experiences of temptation. They may be ashamed of what they write in their dialogues and prefer not to share it with others. This requires you as the leader to be extremely sensitive, both to participants and to the Holy Spirit. If people feel safe enough with one another, it can be powerful for them to read their dialogues out loud to the rest of the group. If you do this, make sure to give them the option not to share if they don't want to. It's safer to have people share their dialogues in pairs, with a prayer partner they trust. Your role is to care for people through this exercise so that they feel safe and supported by the group.

As time goes on, group dynamics tend to either focus on trying not to sin (which becomes stressful) or on helping each other feel better about sin (which becomes stagnant). These are the two pitfalls of legalism and license, which "Next Step: Legalism and License" tries to address. The section titled "Legalism, License, or Love?" invites participants to play a game of noticing these pitfalls in different forms. For those trying to face temptation, these two attitudes are never far away. But ultimately the only cure for legalism *and* license is the love of Jesus, shown to us and through us.

Recommended Reading

○ *The Screwtape Letters* by C. S. Lewis

Session 9. Creating a Battle Plan

Purpose: To create customized, individual strategies for overcoming sexual struggles.

Helpful tips. The main activity, "Strategies for Spiritual Warfare," can be done individually, in pairs, or in a more collaborative format as a larger group. Everyone's plan will look different, and that's a good thing. Receiving copies of these plans will help prayer partners and leaders keep one another accountable not only in avoiding defeat but in putting themselves in a position to experience joy in victory over the obstacles that hold them back from sexual wholeness.

"Next Step: Envision Victory" serves as a follow-up to "Temptation Dialogue." It gives participants an opportunity to use everything they have learned so far in their group. The following section, "A Moment to Pause and Reflect," invites the group as a whole to consider how God has been at work, since the entire process depends on his grace. Use it as an opportunity to practice gratitude and celebrate what God has done, as well as a chance to identify areas for further development.

Creating your battle plan is like writing directions for a road trip. Make the directions as helpful as possible for taking you where you need to go; then follow them. If you need help, ask for it. If you see danger, avoid it. If you take a wrong turn, don't beat yourself up. You don't have to start over, as if the mistake took you back to the place where you started the journey. Simply get back on the right road and continue from where you left off. Even if you swerve off the road, it doesn't do any good to stay in the ditch. Get back on the road, adjust your plan if you need to, and keep going.

Challenges. This session addresses spiritual warfare as a part of sexual recovery. One error would be to underemphasize spiritual warfare by putting all the blame for sexual sin on us (in which case evil is seen only as internal). The opposite error is to overemphasize spiritual warfare by putting all the blame on Satan, demons, and evil spirits (in which case evil is seen as only external). However, a balanced view of spiritual warfare recognizes both the presence of sin at work within us and the presence of spiritual evil at work outside of us. Both sin and "the spiritual forces of evil" (Ephesians 6:12) play a role in sexual temptation.

Creating individual battle plans might overshadow the fact that we are not only able to fight for our own recovery but that we can fight for one another too. We can fight for each other in many ways, including praying for one another, calling to check in, affirming one another, speaking the Word of God to one another, and declaring who we are in Christ.

Don't be discouraged if members of your group seem to be struggling or experiencing relapse. Experts estimate that full recovery from sexual addiction takes two to five years. This journey is not linear, and typically includes many twists and turns along the way. So as your group creates battle plans, remind them that they don't have to come up with a perfect formula. They should expect to readjust the plan as time goes on, especially in response to slips and relapses. Ultimately, we're not just planning for battle but for a lifelong war.

Recommended Reading

◉ *Essentials of Spiritual Warfare* by Scott Moreau

THEME THREE: INTIMACY

Sexuality, our capacity for intimacy in relationships, is part of how we express ourselves as image bearers of the triune God.

God is triune and created us in his image: "In the image of God he created them; male and female he created them" (Genesis 1:27). In other words, God created people as male and female to reflect his communal essence as Father, Son, and Holy Spirit. God created sexuality as a kind of trinitarian self-portrait. Clearly, we are designed for community. Even before sin had entered this world, God said, "It is not good for the man to be alone" (Genesis 2:18). Knowing this reminds us that the path to healthy sexuality is through close relationships with God and others.

Our natural sexual default setting is to take, not to give—to make demands, not to respond to needs. Because we are prone to seek our own self-interests over the interests of others, when sexual desires become more about satisfying ourselves than loving others, the result is lust. This can be true of single, dating, or married people. But the Trinity shows us how to relate to one another in others-centered, selfless, mutually submissive acts of love. This is the ultimate purpose of sexuality: to embody the love of God to/for/with others—that is, to love as God loves. But this is not how we love.

So the opposite of lust is not abstinence; the opposite of lust is Christlike love.

This is why we need to develop our capacity to give and receive love in nonerotic relationships. Our goal in sexuality is to love like Christ.

This means that we must die to self every day. We must trade independence for intimacy. It will be difficult, and sometimes we'll return to selfish patterns. But when we direct our sexual desires to honor and serve others rather than ourselves, we'll discover the beauty of becoming like Christ. It's a tangible way to participate in what the Father, Son, and Spirit have been doing since before the world began.

So sexuality is about *so much more* than having sex; it's our embodied capacity to express the self-giving love of God. More than an avenue for physical pleasure or a desire for romance, sexuality is what drives us out of ourselves to love like God loves. It's our divinely designed engine for intimacy.

Keep in mind, healthy sexuality is not only about what we're avoiding but what we're pursuing, and God created us as sexual people so we would pursue intimacy. Our goal then is to develop authentic intimacy with God and others. We are not called to shut down our sexuality but to cultivate our sexual desires and longings in a holy way.

But we can't practice relationship issues all alone. That is why connecting during the week with prayer partners is so significant. It's in this context that group members learn how to ask for help, give and receive prayer, encourage and challenge each other, and most of all, experience the power of being known and loved for who they are, not who they should be. Living interdependently develops the strength to be single and the maturity to be married.

Note: As group members pursue intimacy with one another, encourage the maintenance of healthy boundaries. True friendship cannot be forced. Beware of "fixers"—participants who help others in order to avoid dealing with their own issues. Help participants focus on their own healing first while still expressing care and concern for others.

Session 10. Healthy Intimacy

Purpose. To pursue intimacy in appropriate ways and develop skills for healthy relationships.

Helpful tips. This session marks a significant transition into talking about what we can and should actually *do* with our sexuality, not just what we are called to avoid but what we are called to pursue positively, right now. The article "Five Types of Intimacy" articulates a more expansive vision for sexuality not confined to erotic behavior and romantic relationships. Because it's so important for participants to wrap their minds around this bigger picture, this session offers a short essay on the subject rather than a specific passage of Scripture. Read it out loud together.

"Next Step: Intimacy Skills" emphasizes how our capacity for intimacy relates to being single *and* to being married. Learning how to satisfy our desires for intimacy in healthy ways helps us to connect with people more meaningfully, whether with a spouse or a close friend. In con-

sidering which character qualities and skills are most important for being single and for being married, hopefully participants will see no lack of similarities between the two.

The following are some ideas for cultivating a stronger sense of intimacy and interdependence in your group.

1. Spend time together in settings and activities totally unrelated to the group. It could be studying, exercising, going out to coffee or lunch, having fun, or just talking about life. This helps to create a group dynamic in which talking about sexual issues isn't the only way you connect with each other.

2. Try taking a break from using the curriculum for a weekly meeting. Allow everyone to have an unstructured conversation, get distracted, joke around, and give longer updates than normal. This can serve as a reminder to prioritize relationships over rules. During an especially taxing time of the year, a more laid-back meeting can give people the relaxation and refreshment they need.

3. Let participants minister to you. Remember that the Holy Spirit can minister *to* them by ministering *through* them. When participants realize that the Holy Spirit can use them to minister to you, the leader, both of you will experience deeper healing. You may even find that the person you reached out to for help now feels comfortable reaching out to *you* for help. That's interdependence.

Our need for intimacy and interdependence makes us a bit like sheep. Sheep need to stay together to survive. Wolves know this, for "the wolf attacks the flock and scatters it" (John 10:12). The plan of Satan, the wolf, is simple: divide and conquer. In contrast, our plan is simple: stay close to your group, the flock, and to Jesus, the good Shepherd.

Challenges. Both the main activity, "Intimacy Needs" and "Next Step: Intimacy Skills" are designed to counteract individualism and promote interdependence. It's extremely difficult to put this into practice, but when groups realize and act on their need for one another, amazing things happen. Do your participants ask each other for help during the week? Do they pray together during times of need? Are they sharing life with people who know and love them deeply? If so, you can expect to see transformation take place. But you can't force intimacy. You *can* model it yourself, emphasize it as appropriate, and have participants share examples of how it has helped them.

Recommended Reading

- *Connecting: Healing Ourselves and Our Relationships* by Larry Crabb

- *Sexuality and Holy Longing: Embracing Intimacy in a Broken World* by Lisa Graham McMinn

Session 11. Christlike Sexuality

Purpose: To consider how we can imitate Jesus' sacrificial, self-giving love as sexual beings.

Helpful tips. The main activity, "Lust Versus Love," is not mainly about arriving at the right answers. It's first and foremost an exercise in asking the right questions. So instead of "What can I get away with in this situation?" we learn to ask, "How can I follow Jesus in this situation?" Don't think of it as a test that participants can pass or fail. Rather, think of it as a chance to practice navigating challenging situations with Christ as the one providing direction. The goal is to put others' interests above our own and see people as subjects, not sexual objects. Lust says, "You're mine! I need to have you because of what you can give me."

Love says, "You're God's! I choose to bless you because of what he has done for me." Notice how by this definition, it is even possible to lust after one's spouse by relating to them selfishly, rather than in Christlike love.

"Next Step: Sexual Injustice" is a relatively short exercise that invites participants to join Jesus in grieving the injustice of human trafficking and the sex trade. For those who use pornography, this exercise reminds us that this behavior contributes to the global demand for sex trafficking. Pornography is not only a personal problem, it's a breach of justice, perpetuating one of the most dehumanizing industries on the planet. If your group seems particularly moved by this issue, consider watching the documentary *Nefarious* during a weekly meeting or getting involved with an organization such as International Justice Mission or Not for Sale.

The idea of Jesus as a sexual person can be confusing, but it's important. In the incarnation of Jesus Christ, God took on the flesh of a sexual human being. Creator became creature. How unthinkable: that God the Son would forsake the privileges of divinity to become a poor, celibate carpenter for our sake, and then stay human, stay embodied, stay sexual for eternity. In Christ, God chose to become a sexual human being and yet to never have sex. This reveals just how good and beautiful sexuality is, *and* how nonessential sex is to our happiness.

Challenges. Talking about the sexuality of Jesus tends to lead to speculation and rabbit trail conversations (for example, Did Jesus ever have a wet dream or masturbate?). As a leader, it's okay to allow space for such curiosity and humor. However, the more important question of "What does Jesus' sexuality have to do with mine?" should not be taken lightly. It can lead to significant insights about Jesus and oneself. Ultimately, this conversation can help people understand what it means to imitate the countercultural, cross-shaped life of Christ. The self-sacrificial shape of Jesus' life challenges our expectations and ambitions for our own sexual fulfillment.

While discussing dating during the main activity, "Lust Versus. Love," participants will probably bring up the age-old question: Where's the line? What baseline physical boundaries should a couple keep before getting married? Although Christlike sexuality cannot be reduced to a matter of maintaining wise physical boundaries, boundaries still play an important role. Encourage participants who are dating to set limits on physical touch, and on late nights in private spaces. You can also help them move beyond trying not to "cross the line" into actively seeking to honor and protect one another.

Recommended Reading

- ○ *Soul Virgins: Reimagining Single Sexuality* by Douglas Rosenau and Michael Todd Wilson

- ○ *Are You Waiting for "the One"?* by Margaret Peterson and Dwight Peterson

- ○ *The Meaning of Marriage* by Tim Keller and Kathy Keller

Session 12. Pursuing Wholeness

Purpose: To integrate what has been learned into a comprehensive, practical vision for sexuality.

Helpful tips. The main activity, "Sexual Wholeness," might seem like a repetition of session nine's main activity, "Strategies for Spiritual Warfare." This one differs by taking the focus off of resisting temptation and placing it on restoring health and strength to different areas of life that affect sexuality.

It may be that some participants will want to continue meeting weekly (with the group or with a prayer partner) after the conclusion of the curriculum. Some want to because they know they need community to keep healing. Others may want to start their own group out of a desire to keep growing and share their learning with others. People often benefit from going through *Redeemed Sexuality* more than once, especially as a leader or coleader of a new group. Other options for further growth include seeing a professional counselor for deeper insight, joining a twelve-step group in your area, or studying sexuality or sexual addiction more formally through one of the organizations listed later under "Recommended Organizations" (see p. 115).

Because this curriculum accommodates peer-to-peer leadership, consider whether you might want to invite anyone in your group to lead their own group in the future. Leading a group would give them an opportunity to serve as ministers of God's love to the sexually broken, even as they themselves continue to heal and grow in their own sexual recovery. Think about inviting one or two participants to consider becoming leaders or coleaders of a future group. Remember that just because an individual is still wrestling with sexual brokenness does not disqualify them from leading another group. That being said, there are probably some people who are still struggling too deeply to take on a leadership role at this time.

Sexual wholeness is ecological. Ecologists know that adding or removing a single part of an ecosystem not only changes part of the system, it changes the entire system. Introducing a new plant or animal species to an environment can have unpredictable effects: it might destroy the environment or make it flourish. In the same way, adding or removing a dating relationship, spiritual discipline, or thought pattern can make huge changes in someone's sexuality. Invite participants to consider what environmental factors are shaping their sexuality. What "invasive species" might they remove? What life-giving element might they introduce?

Challenges. It can be hard for people to imagine what healthy, thriving sexuality actually looks like in all of life. If participants still don't quite seem to get it, don't worry. The full implications of how the gospel transforms sexual brokenness can't be grasped in an entire lifetime, much less in a few weeks. The most this curriculum can hope to do is initiate a lifelong journey of ongoing discipleship in the area of sexuality. People's experiences in this group are just the beginning of a much bigger story.

"Next Step: Setting Goals" invites participants to turn their vision into action, but it can be easy to forget and not follow through. Without discipline supporting the desire to change, people will either plateau or plummet after leaving the group. People in your group may have learned a lot, but if they don't use what they learned, they will lose it. Encourage them to share their goals out loud and hold one another accountable to them, even after the group has dissolved.

Recommended Organizations

- Authentic Intimacy
- Bethesda Workshops
- Celebrate Recovery
- Fight the New Drug
- Harvest USA
- Institute for Sexual Wholeness
- Living Without Lust
- Pure Desire Ministries
- Sex Addiction Treatment Provider Institute
- Sex Addicts Anonymous
- Sex and Love Addicts Anonymous
- Sexaholics Anonymous
- XXXChurch.com

AFTER *REDEEMED SEXUALITY*

Here are some ideas for concluding your group in a meaningful way:

1. Find a time that will work for all of you to have fun and celebrate what God has done. Some groups go to dinner to celebrate. Some gather around a bonfire. Some go on a special excursion. Make your celebration whatever would be most joyful, encouraging, and fitting for your group.

2. Have participants write a letter to themselves. Each participant's "letter to self" will be handed to you as the leader to be sent back to the participant six months after the group has ended. This letter serves two purposes: to remind participants of what God has done in their lives in this area, and to give themselves advice for the future based on what they have learned. The letter should summarize what they want to remember from their time in this group. (Don't forget to gather future addresses and send the letters back to them after six months!) People often forget they wrote these letters and are surprised to receive them in the mail! This can be a powerful, encouraging follow-up.

3. Host a ceremony to commission everyone for life beyond the group. This can include:

- Singing worship songs as a group in response to what God has done and is doing.

- Time for publically, verbally affirming one another (see "Next Step: Practicing Affirmation" in chap. 5).

- Giving a gift or writing a letter to each participant as a token of remembrance. For example: a bracelet with the participant's favorite identity statement on it.

- Rewriting or retelling sexual histories—except this time, instead of framing it as a story of sexual shame and sin, frame it as a story about redemption through the grace of God. Imagine you are looking at your story from God's perspective as you tell it!

ENCOURAGEMENT FOR YOU

As the leader you have run this race to the finish with your eyes on Christ, your ears attentive to the Spirit, and your heart beating with the love of the Father for the people in your group. You made mistakes, but you learned a lot too. And God never wasted a single moment of it. Well done! In your weakness, his power was made perfect (2 Corinthians 12:9). Praise God!

NOTES

AN INVITATION TO THE BROKEN

3   *sexually broken people into an ongoing process of discipleship*: New research from BARNA estimates that only 7 percent of churches have sexual recovery programs. See Barna, *The Porn Phenomenon: The Impact of Pornography in the Digital Age* (Ventura, CA: Barna Group, 2016).

culture does a much better job of this than the church: Juli Slattery, "The Importance of Sexual Discipleship," *Authentic Intimacy*, February 3, 2016, www.authenticintimacy.com/resources/2641 /the-importance-of-sexual-discipleship.

1 LEARNING THE LANGUAGE

13   *the way we experience the healing process*: For special instructions on how to guide personal sharing in your group, see appendix 1, "How to Do Updates."

14   *We are sexual at our core*: Douglas Rosenau and Michael Todd Wilson, *Soul Virgins: Redefining Single Sexuality* (Grand Rapids: Baker, 2006), 30.

15   *unwelcome conduct of a sexual nature*: "Student Life Title IX Policy," "Discrimination, Harassment, and Sexual Misconduct Policy," Wheaton College, January 20, 2017, www.wheaton.edu/~/media/Files /Student-Life/Student-Care/DiscriminationHarassmentSexualMisconductPolicy-lastupdate2017 0126.pdf.

a particular type of sexual harassment: Ibid.

16   *Masturbation teaches us that immediate gratification*: Lauren F. Winner, *Real Sex: The Naked Truth About Chastity* (Grand Rapids: Brazos, 2005), 113.

3 WOUNDS OF THE PAST

28   *Forgiving yourself is accepting the truth*: Neil T. Anderson, *The Steps to Freedom in Christ* (Ventura, CA: Gospel Light, 2001), 19.

prayer is to be spoken: adapted from ibid., 22.

6 THE WOUNDED SELF

48   *Imagine that you could be neurologically "enslaved"*: William Struthers, *Wired for Intimacy* (Downers Grove, IL: InterVarsity Press, 2010), 187.

48-49   *Figure 6.1, sexual core beliefs and figure 6.2, "Cycle of sexual addiction"*: adapted from Mark R. Laaser, *Healing the Wounds of Sexual Addiction* (Grand Rapids: Zondervan, 2004), 60, 108. Laaser cites Patrick J. Carnes, *Out of the Shadows: Understanding Sexual Addiction* (Center City, MN: Hazeldon, 2001), 99-102, as the source of this information.

50   *Figure 6.3, "Cycle of sexual redemption"*: This is an original creation of the author, modifying Carnes's and Laaser's diagrams with his own titles.

10 HEALTHY INTIMACY

76   *categories of intimacy*: Douglas Rosenau and Michael Todd Wilson, *Soul Virgins: Redefining Single Sexuality* (Grand Rapids: Baker, 2006), 190-92.

77   *ten key intimacy needs*: David Ferguson, Teresa Ferguson, Bruce Walker, and Joy Walker, *Discovering Intimacy: Experiencing Great Commandment Love in Single Adult Relationships* (Austin, TX: Intimacy Press, 1984), 38.

11 CHRISTLIKE SEXUALITY

83   *Some facts*: "Sex Trafficking Facts," *Equality Now*, accessed April 27, 2017, www.equalitynow.org /traffickingFAQ.

12 PURSUING WHOLENESS

86   *This process involves developing* spiritual intimacy: Steve Corbett and Brian Fikkert, *When Helping Hurts: How to Alleviate Poverty Without Hurting the Poor—and Yourself* (Chicago: Moody Publishers, 2012), 59.

88   *Think S.M.A.R.T.*: Graham Yemm, *Essential Guide to Leading Your Team: How to Set Goals, Measure Performance and Reward Talent* (Boston: Pearson Education, 2013), 37-39.

APPENDIX 2: PRAYERS FOR THE JOURNEY

95   *these prayers*: With the exception of "The Prayer of Blessing," the prayers in this liturgy are found in "The (Online) Book of Common Prayer," Episcopal Church, accessed May 9, 2017, www.bcponline .org. "The Prayer of Assurance" is slightly modified. "The Prayer of Blessing" is found in *Our Modern Services: Anglican Church of Kenya* (Carrollton, TX: Ekklesia, 2008).

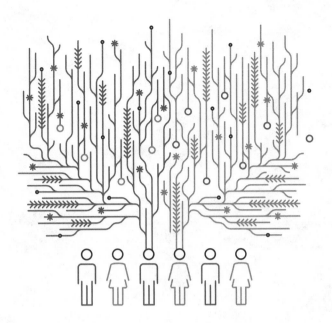

ADDITIONAL RESOURCES